Authenticity

Clearing the Junk:
A Buddhist Perspective

2007
Lantern Books
One Union Square West
Suite 201
New York, NY 10003

Printed in Canada.

Library of Congress Cataloging-in-Publication Data

Yifa.
  Authenticity : Clearing the Junk : A Buddhist Perspective / Yifa.
      p. cm.
  ISBN-13: 978-1-59056-109-6 (alk. paper)
  ISBN-10: 1-59056-109-0 (alk. paper)
  1. Religious life—Buddhism. 2. Religious life—Fo Guang Shan Buddhist Order.
I. Title.
  BQ5405.Y55 2007
  294.3'444—dc22

                              2007016393

Lantern Books has elected to print this title on Legacy TB, a 100% post-consumer recycled paper, processed chlorine-free. As a result, we have saved the following resources:

10.88 trees, 31.43 lbs of water-borne waste, 4,623 gallons of wastewater, 512 lbs of solid
waste, 1,007 lbs of net greenhouse gases, and 7,709,912 BTUs of energy.

As part of Lantern Books' commitment to the environment we have joined the Green
Press Initiative, a nonprofit organization supporting publishers in using fiber that is not
sourced from ancient or endangered forests. We hope that you, the reader, will support
Lantern and the GPI in our endeavor to preserve the ancient forests and the natural systems on which all life depends. One way is to buy books that cost a little more but
make a positive commitment to the environment not only in their words, but in the
paper that they are written on.

For more information, visit www.greenpressinitiative.org.

Authenticity

Clearing the Junk:
A Buddhist Perspective

Venerable Yifa

New York · Lantern Books
A Division of Booklight, Inc.

Contents

Acknowledgments

This book would not have been possible without the forethought and diligent work of my editor and publisher at Lantern Books, Martin Rowe. He worked with me on *Safeguarding the Heart*, my first book with Lantern, as well as the revised version, *The Tender Heart*, and has been a longtime supporter of my writing, as well as being the publisher of two of the Venerable Master Hsing Yun's books, *Living Affinity* and *Opening the Mind's Eye*.

I also wish to express my gratitude to the Venerable Master Hsing Yun, for the almost thirty years I have spent with Fo Guang Shan, and for his concern for my spiritual wellbeing and career.

Introduction

This little book is about junk: the things we fill our lives and occupy our time with, but which provide us with little sustenance; the thoughts and emotions that distract us, cause us and others consternation or trouble, and over which we seem to have no control.

I am approaching this topic from what might be seen as an unusual perspective. For almost three decades I have been a nun with a Taiwan-based Buddhist organization called Fo Guang Shan ("Buddha's Light Mountain"), which teaches what our founder the Venerable Master Hsing Yun calls "Humanistic Buddhism." As the name suggests, Humanistic Buddhism aims to make Buddhism relevant to people's everyday concerns. It also hopes to provide individuals with spiritual tools that will allow them to negotiate the great passages of their lives—birth, marriage, children, and death—with equanimity and courage.

During my years as a nun I've taught students and members of the public about Buddhist history and practice in Taiwan and in the United States. Even though I myself don't have many material possessions, have shaved my head and taken a vow of celibacy, and have lived a relatively simple life, simply by shuttling between Taiwan and America and visiting many other countries throughout the world, I've been exposed to my fair share of junk. Students have come to me because they're in junk relationships and want to get out of them. People have expressed dismay to me at how they've accumulated so much stuff over the years. And some have become addicted to drugs and alcohol and put other junk in their bodies. In the course of my life, moreover, I've seen the explosive growth of junk food and what I consider to be junk culture, and I've been the cause and victim of junk communication—mindless and superficial conversation or email that has placed information before knowledge and data before wisdom, and has simply wasted a lot of time and energy.

It is my belief that Buddhism offers valuable lessons that we can apply in order to control junk in our lives and take back some of the mental, spiritual, and physical integrity that has been lost in the madcap rush to accumulate and accomplish more and more things. I'm under no illusion as to how hard this is. In the modern world, many of us are very wired. We're either high on artificial stimulants like coffee or alcohol or cocaine or some other "sensation," or we're hooked up to music or video systems, personal digital assistants, cell phones, and the other paraphernalia of instant communication. The irony is that in spite of all the things that tell us what we have to do and when we have to do it, our information overload is making us forget who or where we are, why we're here, and where we're going. We "know" so much that we no longer have any idea of what we know in our hearts. We're so bombarded with people telling us what to buy that we can no longer tell what is of genuine value and what is, well, junk. We're so preoccupied, distracted, and multi-tasked that we can no longer work out what we want to do with our lives or really pay attention to the people we care about. We're in such a hurry to get from one meeting to another, one person to another, or one deal to another that in those very rare moments when we have nothing to do and no one to meet, we panic: What are we going to do with ourselves? For one moment, we sit in a kind of daze. The next moment we reach for some kind of umbilical cord to the outside world: we log on, dial up, check in, tune out, and distract ourselves all over again.

I'm not going to pretend that I, or this little book, have all the answers. I'm also not going to suggest that the way to stop our junk-filled lives from spinning completely out of control is for all of us to become monastics. Indeed, some of the busiest and most over-scheduled people I know are monks and nuns! I, too, love to travel and communicate the glories and wisdom of our religious tradition. Like many people, I've been able to do this because I live in a post-industrial, high-tech world that has made communication and travel affordable and available to more people than ever before (even though we're beginning to see the costs to the planet and our lives that the supposedly cost-free existence of international travel is exacting).

I know that I benefit from the modern world. In addition to flying to many countries and parts of the United States and driving a car, I live in places where there is heat and running water, and the water I drink is clean. I don't have to worry about whether I'll be able to eat or whether that food will be enough for me. I value the information I receive from the various media. I gain pleasure from watching films and reading books and I enjoy the experience of travel, both actual and vicarious, that technology allows me. This book was written on a computer and I communicated with my editor and publisher by email. So, I don't want to suggest that all the conveniences we surround ourselves with are inherently bad for us. As with so much in Buddhism, it is our *attitude* toward these things and how we *use* what has been produced for us that matters.

All I'm saying, perhaps over modestly, is that at times it helps to get off the out-of-control roller coaster that our life may be taking us on and think about what is truly valuable to us. Then, once we decide to get back on the roller coaster, we'll be better able to react to the inevitable ups and downs and handle more calmly the speed and nausea that such rides may give us. When we have more tools to cope with what life presents us with, we also become better people: more thoughtful, considerate, even more tolerant. This is a function of controlling the way we think and speak, and not being hostage to thinking and feeling that causes us and other people pain and grief.

Buddhism is not only very practical about human needs and desires, it's also very honest and generous about us as human beings. It recognizes that life is not, to put it mildly, a bed of roses, and that our needs and desires often cloud our judgment, both about what we have done and what remains to be done. Buddhism understands that right and wrong are often matters of perspective and context, and that the great questions of life—Who are we? Why are we here?—may not be answered in the course of our life, but that they may extend over many lifetimes and adopt many forms. Even after many generations, the answers may still elude us.

Buddhism began over 2,500 years ago, when the prince-turned-mendicant Siddhartha Gautama became an awakened being and gathered disciples around him to learn the secrets of being enlightened. The disciplines he established then branched out into a rich and vivid set of reflections on what it means to be alive and how best to respond to life's challenges. Throughout this time, Buddhism has concerned itself not only with the big issues but also with the more modest but no less significant goal of providing techniques of thinking and practice (such as meditation) that settle the dust clouds of confusion in our head. The aim is to create a mind of clarity and serenity, so that in any given situation that may confront us in our life, we can ascertain what the true nature of that situation is and deal with it with the least amount of harm and suffering to anyone or anything—or us. And it is from this perspective of Buddhist practice that I write about junk.

1 ❋ Food

We've forgotten how to eat.

That might seem an odd statement, since—at least in the industrialized world—food seems to be everywhere. We can go into a supermarket in Beijing and Tokyo, Los Angeles and New York, London, Paris, and Moscow and select from what seem to be innumerable brands of cereal. We can choose from enormous piles of fruits and vegetables shipped from all over the world; we can purchase huge containers of juice, soda, beer, and other drinks; we can fill our trolleys with big bags of chips and bottomless jars of cookies, and try to save money on so-called value packs of all manner of things. Never in the history of the planet have so many of us had so much access to such bounty at one time.

We also seem to have no problem remembering that we need to eat. There are over one thousand McDonald's restaurants in China and seven thousand in Europe. From Riyadh to Cape Town there are multinational food chains and other fast-food outlets on almost every corner, reminding us that a meal is but a few minutes and a few dollars away. Stroll down the street in any major city and the restaurants serving cuisine from all over the world are full of people. And when we aren't in restaurants, we're wrapping our mouths around huge sandwiches as we rush to and from work, travel on the subway, or sit in our offices. Everywhere you look, it seems, we're snacking or grazing or nibbling. We're also eating bigger portions and more often. No wonder people in the industrialized world (and the rich in the developing countries) are getting fatter and fatter.

What I mean when I say that we've forgotten how to eat is that we've lost a sense of the *meaning* of food. Eating should not be about stuffing ourselves with fat and sugar, or piling on the protein or calories. Eating should be about consuming healthy and nutritious food, prepared with care and love, and sharing it with one's family or friends in a mood of joy and celebration.

Let's be honest: How often is a reverence for food and the process of preparing it a true reflection of our lives? How often do we find ourselves hunched over our desks at work, with only our computer monitors as our lunch companions? How often do we skip a healthy breakfast in favor of a mid-morning snack of coffee and a sandwich or bagel eaten as we run to our office? How often do we reach for the antiacids because we've eaten our food (which was too rich for us in the first place) too quickly and have gotten indigestion or heartburn? Or how often do we have to take laxatives or anti-diarrhea medicine because our food doesn't contain enough fiber or has been prepared so carelessly that it's infected with a food-borne disease? How often do we turn off the television or DVD player and sit down with our loved ones at a table and share the news of the day with each other? How often do we thank the person who prepared the food, the farmer who grew it, the many people and the technology that delivered it to the vendor from whom we bought it? How often do we give thanks to whatever deity or spiritual being we worship, or express gratitude in whatever discipline we practice, for giving us such abundance in the first place?

Increasingly, so it seems, these days few of us do any of the above, let alone all of them. In our hectic modern world, there's a tendency to take food for granted, just as we've come to assume that we can eat fresh produce no matter what the weather is like outside, what season it is, or which country the food comes from. We fill ourselves with calories and fuel and then we're off to the next thing.

It is a marvel that we can taste cuisines from all over the world and have such abundance. Yet we rarely stop to consider how lucky we are. And even though we're surrounded by so much, many of us are still not happy. We pound away on the treadmills or the stationary bikes in the gym, convinced that if we spent a little time working out we'd attain the perfect body. Or we go on diets that tell us to eat only carbohydrates or restrict them, to drink only juices or consume more greens, cut out meat or have more of it. We're lactose-intolerant, wheat gluten–averse, and allergic to nuts. Our food supply is contaminated with E. coli, Salmonella, Campylobacter, and chemicals that we're told are carcinogenic. Now we're being warned to watch out for trans-fats and high fructose corn syrup in the foods because they're bad for us, but which are hard to resist precisely because those same substances make them tasty in the first place. We want to look like the celebrities we see in the junk magazines that sit next to the junk candy and cookies by the cash register in the supermarket. But even some of these very same celebrities, with all their wealth and prestige, aren't happy. They, too, are either on their special diets, relentlessly relayed to us through these same magazines, or they're having anti-aging toxins pumped into their bodies or altering them through plastic surgery. Like the celebrities, some of us spend a considerable amount of time and a lot of money trying to be perfect, to take a few pounds off here and tone ourselves there. And yet it never seems to be enough.

How did we get this way? Partly, of course, it's the task of the advanced capitalist economies some of us live in to make us feel perpetually unsatisfied. We're thrifty animals at heart, concerned with scarcity and genetically predisposed to eat what is there before us, even though we may no longer be hungry, rather than risk the possibility of going without food for a long time. We're also social creatures, concerned with fitting in and not being left behind by the pack. So we're constantly and anxiously on the lookout for trends that will make us both distinctive within the group and yet fully part of it—worried, as we are, that we won't be able to compete with our peers in the social marketplace. Advertisers know this very well; that's why they're constantly trying to persuade us that we're getting value for our money. We rush to the all-you-can-eat buffet and fill ourselves with more and more food as though we'll never have a chance to eat again. We buy the value-pack or "supersized" version of something even though a few short years ago we would have settled quite happily for a single item that now comes in a pack of six, or a small version of a drink that's now double or even triple the size. We ask for extra toppings, double scoops, or more side orders. When the plates arrive, piled high with an impossibly large amount of food, we laugh and tell our dinner companions that we cannot believe how huge the portions are these days. And then we proceed to clean the plate.

Of course, I am exaggerating. But if you recognize anything of yourself or your society in what I've described, then you'll probably agree that I'm not exaggerating by much. We live with such abundance and such profligacy. And yet we seem so anxious and dissatisfied.

The Buddha understood the importance of having a healthy attitude toward food. After leaving the luxurious palace he was brought up in so he could begin his search for enlightenment, Siddhartha Gautama practiced a rigorous asceticism. For six years he fasted, until he became so thin that, as legend has it, he could touch his belly and feel his backbone. He looked almost like a skeleton. However, at some point, he realized that his attitude toward food wasn't leading him to enlightenment but, instead, was preventing him from finding it. In short, he'd become emotionally attached to the very process of denial that he was practicing in order to overcome attachment.

This is somewhat analogous to those unfortunate people who suffer from anorexia nervosa or bulimia. In their minds they have an image of how they'd like their bodies to be—one that may bear no relation to their current reality or even to any idea of genuine health, or that exists within the (admittedly often negative or unachievable) contemporary, Western norms of beauty. The anorexic and bulimic then starve themselves or manipulate their food intake in a way that makes them feel both disgusted and pleased with themselves. This gives them a false sense of control over their lives even as they become more and more controlled by their addiction.

The Buddha saw that the path to enlightenment didn't lie in extreme asceticism, just as it couldn't be found in self-indulgence and thoughtless luxury. Instead, it lay in recognizing that we have basic needs—to be fed and sheltered—and that this moderate, Middle Way needs to be satisfied. You can see how our body understands its needs when those who haven't eaten for a long time find it hard to hold down their food because their stomachs have shrunk. Our bodies have to be fed regularly, even if the amount we consume is small. Food cannot be denied to us; we need to eat. Yet we cannot eat too much, since obesity and its consequences—glaucoma, diabetes, heart attacks, strokes, and other conditions—can also be deadly for us.

Once the Buddha realized he couldn't starve himself to enlightenment, he washed himself in the river and accepted an offering of goat's milk. Can you imagine how delicious that first drink must have tasted? Can you imagine how much the Buddha valued that offering and how grateful he must have been to the woman who gave him the goat's milk? Even if we can't express that level of gratitude for each bite or sip we take, if we could capture just a fraction of that thankfulness and pleasure in our daily life when it comes to food, then we'd no doubt open ourselves up to the enormous riches that are found in recognition and appreciation, and have a healthier attitude toward food.

One way I try to encourage my students to think sensibly about food is by making them concentrate on something that's perhaps undertaken with even less thought than the eating of food and the drinking of liquid; and that's the eliminating of both. I call it "the philosophy of the toilet." I suggest to my students that, when they get up each morning and go to sit on the toilet, they take a moment to feel grateful for their body. It is our body that works every second of every minute of every hour of a day, processing what we ingest and attempting to compensate for our abuse. And all without our telling it to do anything. It is our body that allows us to get rid of the waste and create more space so we can put more food and drink into it. When we're very sick and we lose our appetite, we feel wretched; we don't want food and our bowel movements become irregular. Many cancer patients cannot eat, not because they're not able to take in food, but because they cannot eliminate the waste.

Thus, what we consider the cycle of ingestion and elimination is also a balance: between what we need and what we no longer need; between what is about to be good for us and what is no longer good for us. This is why we should be full of forethought and care about what we put in our bodies. As the Vietnamese Buddhist monk Thich Nhat Hanh has recognized in his writings, the heart and transformative power of that food lies in the gathering of the sun and the rain and the fertility of the soil and the generation of the seed. In *Dharma Rain*, he offers a blessing: "In this food, I see clearly the presence of the entire universe supporting my existence."

One area that is often overlooked when we think about food is the act of chewing. Chewing helps our enzymes break down food more efficiently and for better health. In our fast-paced world, however, we don't spend enough time chewing and savoring our food. Indigestion and stomach pain seem an uncomfortable price to pay for convenience. There's a philosophical component here as well: we don't spend enough time chewing over problems or ruminating. If we waited a few moments and let the food sit in our mouths, or waited for an idea to develop or a problem to dissolve using the enzymes of our meditative mind, then we might be able to take apart something indigestible and turn it into something nourishing and delicious. If we chewed over things a little more then we might find decisions and outcomes we could stomach!

One way the world's religious traditions have forced us to appreciate the bounty of food and the natural pacing of our digestive system when it is working properly is through controlled fasting. In some Buddhist traditions, lay people who are interested in experiencing the monastic life visit the temple for training in "restraint and fasting." They live in the monastery for a day and a night once or sometimes several times a month. During this time they're required to keep a fast after midday.

The origin of this practice according to the *Vinaya*, or the Buddhist scriptures, is from the time of the Buddha, when Kalodayin, one of the Buddha's disciples, showed up at a household one afternoon collecting alms (which is how the very earliest Buddhist monks lived). The wife of the house, who was heavily pregnant, opened the door to offer food to Kalodayin. However, at that very moment, a lightning strike lit up the sky and the woman was so shocked that she miscarried the child. From then on, the Buddha retrained the monastics so they wouldn't need to seek alms or food after midday.

Besides the fasting in the afternoon, lay people at the monastery are obligated to follow the five precepts of Buddhism—no killing, no stealing, no sexual misconduct, no lying, and no intoxicants. They're asked not to wear adornments such as perfume or flowers, to resist watching entertainments, and to avoid luxury bedding and seating. The idea is to cultivate a life of simplicity and non-attachment. Many visitors enjoy the time they spend at the monastery. They see it as a chance to regain some balance in their lives, and to focus their mind on what is valuable to them. They recognize, like the Buddha, that the point of fasting shouldn't be to deny ourselves everything so we're incapable of performing basic functions and operating at our full potential. It's precisely the opposite: to allow us to experience gratitude for all we have and enable us to do all we wish with clear intention and a pure mind.

It's significant, I believe, that many of the world's religions encourage periods of restraint and self-control. I've always been impressed by the discipline within the Islamic and Christian traditions of Ramadan and Lent. During Ramadan, devout Muslims don't eat or drink from sunrise to sunset. They also abstain from sex. During Lent, some Christians also fast and practice restraint in their conduct, as well as perform acts of penance. Beyond the specifics of each faith's tradition, the point of both Ramadan and Lent is to make us grateful for what we have, to acknowledge that all bounty comes from God, and to realize that our lives gain depth and perspective when we practice discipline and hold off from indulging our appetites—so that we may appreciate our freedom and pleasure that much more. The Jewish concept of Sabbath and Jubilee, where every seventh day and every fiftieth year human beings are commanded not to work and to let the ground lie fallow, is also a recognition that we should take the necessary time to acknowledge bounty and honor God, and give that which produces that abundance a chance to recuperate and be renewed.

The Buddha realized that extreme asceticism was an impediment to spiritual growth. However, in beginning to consume food and drink again, the Buddha wasn't saying we should become gluttonous or not worry about the sources of food. The Buddha was deeply concerned with not killing—it is one of the five main precepts of Buddhist doctrine—which is why many Buddhist orders are vegetarian. He also understood that while food should be savored and appreciated, it shouldn't be fetishized, even though Buddhist temple cuisine can be highly refined and prepared with great care. What the Buddha wanted from his adherents was to focus the attention on every aspect of life so it could be seen for what it was. Junk, to the contrary, blocks our attention by making us focus on the object in an unhealthy way. How this happens will become clearer in later chapters in this book.

When we sit down to eat in our monastery at Fo Guang Shan, we try to be conscious of several things. We eat in silence because this way you can concentrate on the food and practice awareness. Then we eat everything that has been prepared for us on the plate. This is our way of honoring the conservation of resources. We also try to make sure that the conservation of resources takes place before the food even reaches our plate: the portions we receive aren't too large, and this way it isn't difficult to eat all that's been given to us. We also remember the preparation of the food—the work of the cooks and the cleaners and those who picked the vegetables and processed the food. We don't choose what we eat at the monastery. We're not in the monastery to become gourmands. We're there because we need to cultivate appreciation and non-attachment to all things, including food.

These ritual behaviors are part of what we call the "five contemplations." The first contemplation is to develop **gratitude**. We give thanks for the food and how it came to us. We reflect on the food's growth from seed to flowering plant, its harvesting and journey from the fields to the market; then we appreciate its arrival and preparation in the kitchen, and the effort it took to supply this food. We acknowledge the interdependence of all natural things—how they work together in harmony to bring us what is nutritious and life-giving. We recognize, too, that life forms may have been harmed in the gathering of this food (even though we don't eat meat, we know that animals may have been disturbed by the harvesting of the vegetables, fruits, and grains) and we honor the gifts they've made to us.

The second contemplation is to develop **humility**. In the monastery we're privileged in that we don't pay money for our meals. However, we know the meal is not cost free. We're also aware that many in the world don't have access to any food, no matter what the price. It's a great blessing to us that we have people who cook for us and prepare the tables. We're always at risk of taking them for granted—just as, in society as a whole, we take for granted the people who work in the factories or the migrant laborers who pluck our fruits and vegetables from the trees and bushes or pull them up from the ground. That we forget all those who work out of sight for our comfort is an unfortunate tendency in our culture. The second contemplation forces us, therefore, at least for a moment, to be aware that they exist and that we should be grateful for them. Perhaps such gratitude might make us more likely to help these laborers as they advocate for better work and living conditions.

The point of the second contemplation is to reflect on one's own virtue and to understand that, unlike the Buddha with that first gift of goat's milk, we may be morally deficient when we receive the offering. This is exemplified by the fact that we've lost sight of gratitude in our culture, especially when it comes to the act of "saying grace" over our meals.

I remember on one occasion, I was eating with a young man who asked: "If I paid five dollars for this meal, why do I still have to say 'thank you'?"

"Do you think that your five dollars really *bought* this meal?" I asked him. "Let's count up the economic cost that led to this food coming together in this form for you. Think about all the causes and conditions that were involved in terms of time and space for this set of ingredients to be cooked in such a way and then be available to eat." And so the young man and I did just that. I can't remember the exact number we came up with, but the amount of money and the perhaps unquantifiable effort involved were considerably more than what he paid. The young man ate a bit of humble pie with his meal that day!

The third contemplation we perform is to develop **restraint**. Restraint means protecting the integrity of our mind so that we're less likely to depart from our discipline and avoid errors, as well as not be greedy. So, not only should we not take more than we need, but we should always practice consideration in making sure that everyone has what they need. We must be aware not to become selfish, indulge our tastes, and wish to take more than our share—whether it's in piling our plate high, or making it so that other people don't get enough to eat. We must be appreciative of people's efforts. We shouldn't ask why we were given the food, complain about the taste, or disparage the skills of those who prepared it. We should accept it with gratitude and grace, thanking everyone involved for their work and care.

The fourth contemplation is the generation of **health-providing thoughts about the food**. We should sense it nourishing us and giving us energy and vitality, coursing through our bodies. That's why the food in the monastery should always be nutritious. The food prepared should be good for the digestion, soft on the palate, and flavorful. There's no reason why it should be devoid of taste or pleasure. The Chinese monastic tradition considers food and medicine to be from the same source. Food is always cooked using herbs and spices together to combine taste, nutritional value, and the healing power of those herbs and spices. This is a different conception of food from the West, where nutrition has, until relatively recently, not been thought of as a key component in preventing disease and curing ailments. The fourth contemplation allows us to consider food as a medicinal force.

The fifth contemplation aims to encourage **examination of the purpose of our lives**. The entire process of sitting down to eat, reflecting on food and its preparation, and then the eating of it should be a method—one among many—to take us further on the path to enlightenment. This again is why the food in our temples is vegetarian: because we want to emphasize the life-giving nature of food and to discourage the taking of life.

During the time of the Buddha, monks and nuns lived

in the forests or hills, only coming to the villages to walk from house to house seeking food. Even though Buddhists were themselves not allowed to kill, they weren't allowed to refuse any food that was given to them, even if that food contained meat. There were, however, certain proscriptions. Buddhists weren't allowed to eat the flesh of any animal that they had seen or heard killed, or which had been slaughtered specifically for them. These were known as the "three kinds of impure meat." The proscriptions were established so that, when the monks entered the household where they were to receive the food, they wouldn't be thinking of the newly killed animal, and thus have an image of the slaughtered beast in their mind—therefore weighing the monk down with a karmic burden that would make it harder for him to cultivate compassion. Other proscriptions were that Buddhists shouldn't eat an elephant or a horse, since they were considered royal animals. They couldn't scavenge for dead animals in the forest, nor could they take the flesh of any animal in the forest. The thinking was that if they ate the meat, their body would smell like dead flesh, and attract predators such as lions, tigers, leopards, or others.

Over the course of the centuries, as Buddhism ceased to be a religion of wandering mendicants seeking food and became temple-based and self-sustaining, the various branches of Buddhism throughout Asia began to develop their own cuisine. In Chinese culture, because the monastics didn't leave the compound to seek alms, they did all their cooking in the monastery kitchen. Since no animals could be killed for the monks and they couldn't see or hear an animal being slaughtered, the food was naturally completely vegetarian. The Buddhist temple cuisine, which often uses meat analogues such as tofu, seitan, and tempeh, is world-renowned, and these meat analogues are used extensively in Chinese culture and in Asian Buddhist restaurants.

Buddhism does not demand vegetarianism—indeed, Buddhism does not *demand* anything at all. It establishes certain practices that first the Buddha and then his followers saw as helpful in the cultivation of the individual so that she or he might achieve the ultimate goal, which was to gain enlightenment. Thus, vegetarianism was, and is, not an absolute doctrine, which is why not all Buddhists are vegetarian. However, what Buddhism does make clear is that eating meat is very karmically loaded, and thus can be a major stumbling block along the path to compassion and enlightenment. In the process of eating meat, we ingest the fear and suffering of the animals—literally, since the chemicals released when an animal experiences fear remain in the muscles (i.e. the meat) of the animal after the animal has been slaughtered. But there's also a karmic attachment to the food when it's the result of the death of an animal, especially one that has suffered. Therefore, aside from all the environmental, public health, and animal welfare reasons why a plant-based diet is desirable, one should also recognize that meat contains the detritus of death. It makes sense, therefore, that, when we can, we should practice a vegetarian diet. That said, an obsessive attitude toward any kind of diet, vegetarian or otherwise, also causes mental obstruction, because it removes us from the proper task of eating—which is to focus on the goal of achieving *nirvana*, or freedom from desire, hatred, and delusion.

The Buddha realized that it was the mind that governed appetitiveness and greed and hatred, and that only the mind could eliminate it. He understood that his asceticism wasn't cleansing his mind so much as torturing his body, and that whatever he might do to control his need to eat or drink—whether exposing himself to the sun or freezing in the snow or hanging upside down from a tree limb—it was still all about the body. He realized that to keep his mind at peace he needed to satisfy the elementary needs of the body. He also knew that simply sitting all day wouldn't sustain it either. From this wisdom, and that of the Daoist and Hindu traditions, the martial and physical arts—such as Taiji, Qigong, yoga, and others—developed. All of them attempt to move the breath energy, the *qi* or *prana*, around the body in as efficacious and healing a way as possible. These healing arts not only keep the body healthy, but they also promote the kind of mental wellbeing that enables the mind to concentrate and become balanced.

This is why junk food and its corollaries—the wanton use of plastic and bariatric surgery and bizarre diets, or steroids to bulk us up or diuretics to make us thinner—are so misdirected. They may lead us to the emergency room but they won't lead us to happiness. We are, after all, going to die, and our body will one day fail. That is inevitable. No matter how much surgery we undergo, money we have, or restrictive diet we put our stomachs through, we will one day leave this body behind and be reincarnated in another one. But that doesn't mean that the body is a meaningless vessel to be abused or scorned. On the contrary, it means we should honor its needs and seek to sustain it in as healthy and balanced a way as possible, freeing us to concentrate on the task of our lifetimes, which is to remove ourselves from the inevitable death and rebirth of our bodies in the endless karmic cycle.

Enlightenment does not lie in junk food. The latter's promise to make us feel full and feel fulfilled is as empty as its calories. True happiness doesn't lie in stuffing ourselves or eliminating things from our bodies or manipulating them to fit an ideal. Indeed, I would suggest that doing such things only increases our alienation from ourselves and makes us dislike ourselves even more. Instead, we need to honor our appetite, to relish and savor and be grateful for what we have, but eat and drink in such a way that we can move on to working on the mental constructs we have about our bodies and discover what it truly means to be happy.

2 ❋ Stuff

It's an experience that many of us in the industrialized world have had at some point in our lives: we've run out of room. Our closets are full; our cupboards and dressers are stuffed; and our garages, basements, and lofts are overflowing. We've piled things up, bought filing cabinets and storage lockers, and wondered whether we should hire a personal organizer. But we can't escape it: everywhere we look there's more junk than we can handle.

Let's imagine a couple: Bob and Jennifer. In the same way they don't quite know how they managed to put on twenty pounds over the years, so they don't quite understand how their house became so full of things. They don't consider themselves to be shopaholics or hoarders. They're not like those people who keep every issue of *National Geographic* magazine or copies of the *New York Times* piled up in their dusty apartments. They don't spend their time surfing the Shopping Network and they're not impulsive or, they like to imagine, easily swayed by the latest fashion or what a celebrity is wearing that summer. Instead, so they tell themselves, they are judicious and sophisticated purchasers, who only buy what is absolutely necessary for them to live comfortable lives. It's just, somehow, the available real estate for the stuff in their house has shrunk, or closet space isn't what it used to be, or their partner is messier than they thought possible. It's all just baffling.

Do any of Bob and Jennifer's "problems" sound familiar? I began the previous paragraph by comparing the couple's putting on of twenty pounds in weight with the stuff they'd accumulated. It seems to me there's a deeper connection. The global crisis of obesity that is affecting the affluent, or those who live in affluent societies, is at least partly a result of people using food to wall themselves off against the world. Somehow, some of these individuals think that if they stuff themselves they'll not only feel less empty but will be buffered against the shocks and vicissitudes that inevitably come our way. Likewise, they feel that buying more and more things will somehow protect them from that condition that many in the industrial and post-industrial world suffer from: boredom. They divert themselves with things because they worry that if they spent any time with themselves, they'd see how hollow and meaningless their lives were.

This may seem harsh, but Buddhism sometimes has to

ask tough questions of our lives so we break through the comfort zones we like to live in and deal honestly with our needs and who we are. We need to ask ourselves how many pairs of shoes or pants or skirts we really need before we feel good about how we look; how many technical gadgets or latest gizmos we must buy before we feel we're ultra-modern; how many bedrooms we must have in our huge house or how many cars we must acquire before we'll feel rich enough or as good as (or better than) our neighbors; how new or fashionable all this stuff has to be before we'll be satisfied or feel that we have a grasp on contemporary life.

The answer, of course, is that if we judge our self-worth in terms of our material possessions, just as if we eat to fill a spiritual hunger, we'll never consume enough. Some of that hunger, of course, comes from the modern capitalist consumerist society that is both a cause and an effect of our need to satiate ourselves. This society is based on two principles: first, that we're all consumers and we must never feel we have enough goods because then we'll not buy more; secondly, that the products we buy must be obsolete or out-of-date as soon as possible so we're obligated in some way to buy the newer version. We can never escape the dissatisfactions of the consumerist society; it depends on us feeling inadequate and unfulfilled. I get a glimpse of this every time I walk through a department or grocery store. As I see row upon row of clothes, or huge piles of fruit and vegetables, I wonder to myself how the store deals with all the clothes left over from the previous season or the food that's left over from the previous day. Some of this, I know, is taken to homeless shelters or pulped and used for pet food, or sent to the developing world as a charitable donation or a tax write-off. But much of it, I also know, is simply thrown away or recycled. I say to myself: There must be a better way.

Being rich and poor are relative terms. Someone may have very few things but feel rich, because they have fulfilling relationships, enough food to eat, and enough clothes and shelter to feel protected against the elements. Conversely, someone may feel poor even though they have many possessions simply because they don't have as much as some other people. When we need more, no matter how rich we are, we're always poor. When we need less, no matter how poor we are, we're always rich. The hungrier we are for stuff, the more stuff we need; and when we're self-contented, then we can lose everything and still feel we have enough.

Now, we should be careful not to glamorize poverty. There is, of course, genuine need and desperation in many places around the world. However, beyond the basic necessities of life, and the ability to fulfill our potential and maintain positive relationships with our family, neighbors, and community, our attitude to material things becomes a matter of perspective and our sense of who we are as individuals. (We also transfer a lot of our emotional needs and anxieties onto things and possessions, so much so that we lose sight of our identity.)

It is, of course, also true that people have bought from and sold things to people for millennia, and there is genuine skill, artistry, and creativity in the creation of many objects. I'm not opposed to trade or merchandizing on a large scale; mass production and mass consumption stimulate the economy and provide jobs for people. But buying guns to shoot someone and building prisons also stimulate economic activity and few would think those are desirable things for a society to have. We need to be more discriminating. Furthermore, when it comes to consuming products, we need to recognize that we live on a finite planet with finite resources. We may live in a robust global economy at the moment, but the signs are there that this cannot continue indefinitely. We'll need to change how we do business soon, or the planet will do it for us—and at much greater cost to us than if we do it ourselves. There will be more on this subject later on in the chapter.

Buddhism has no intrinsic problem with the getting or spending of money. What is important in Buddhism is our *attachment* to things and not the things in themselves. This is a function of the awareness that everything is interconnected, and that all matter is codependent and co-arising (in other words, there is nothing that pre-originated everything else). Thus money possesses a neutral energy that, depending on the intention of the person who has it, can be used to generate good karma or bad.

A story will exemplify how one might approach the

spending of money. A few years ago I had a conversation with a friend who was a multi-millionaire. "Yifa," he said. "You've been a nun for twenty-four years, and in all that time you haven't worn nice clothes or shoes. That's such a shame."

I smiled at him. "So what are you going to do about it?" I asked.

"I can buy you one hundred pieces of clothing, and then I'll buy you the shoes to go with them. You'll also need a hat, and some accessories such as jewelry."

"All right," I said, interested in seeing how the conversation would continue. "But even if you give me a closet full of clothes and shoes and drawers full of accessories, you still cannot help me with another problem. Every morning for the last twenty-four years I've not had to worry about what I'm going to wear. I just put on my monastic robe and my monastic shoes. Why should I start to make trouble for myself where I didn't have any before?"

Of course, my friend had no way to answer that question, because I was placing my personal satisfaction before material items and simple accumulation, and he had no answer beyond giving me stuff. My friend wasn't bad to want to offer to buy me things, even though he knew I was a nun. I also wanted to make sure that he could see that I appreciated he was offering a gift, and I could see that his *intention* was generous and altruistic. As far as I could tell, he didn't want to court my favor or good opinion. He was simply expressing in a way he knew how that he valued our friendship and thought I'd like these things.

Likewise, I didn't feel that in rejecting his offer I was being churlish or ungrateful. I didn't secretly want to go out on a shopping spree with my friend and felt guilty or resentful in rejecting his offer. Nor do I not admire beautiful things and appreciate the craftsmanship and care that has goes into creating them. Indeed, many Buddhist temples, including those of Fo Guang Shan, are feasts for the eyes, with their vivid colors, gems, beautiful statues, and artful designs. But these temples, like the great cathedrals and mosques that adorn many parts of the world, weren't created to make money or arouse people's envy. They were built to stimulate a sense of reverence and awe, and provide for all worshippers an experience of beauty and tranquility.

What I did with my friend was make a simple calculation: that the increase in my material possessions would not only be a distraction to what I consider to be important in my life (simplicity) but would in fact become an impediment to my equanimity. I'd find myself caught in a trap of having to be at the service of my possessions rather than them serving me. He realized what I was saying, and we both left the conversation a little wiser.

If there's one thing we can be sure of, it's this. Throughout the course of our life, we'll have appetites we'll never satisfy, desires that will never be sated, and needs that will never be met. Even when we're satisfied, it's in our natures to desire more.

A story I once heard exemplifies this well. There was a fisherman, who was known for his skill at angling. He always knew where to catch the fish, but he always did so from the riverbank. This puzzled people, and they'd ask him: "We see that you're very good at fishing. Why don't you buy a boat?"

"Why should I buy a boat?" the man said.

"Because you're so good at fishing. You could make a lot of money."

"And what would I do then?" the fisherman asked.

"You could buy another boat, and make even more money," said the people.

"And what would I do then?"

"You could buy a third boat, and then a fishing fleet. You'd make even more money."

"And what would I do then?" repeated the fisherman.

"Well," said the people, "you could make so much money that you could retire and not have to work again."

"And what would I do then?" asked the man.

"Then you could spend all day fishing."

The old man looked at them. "But that's what I'm doing now."

This story is instructive because it not only suggests that most of us go through life not acknowledging natural limits—after all, to take this story literally, by constantly trying to catch more fish we're depleting the waters of their marine life—but that we often work simply to accumulate money and stuff rather than think about what we're working and living *for*. The man knows his limitations, and that he doesn't need a boat. He works to get only what he needs to live, and he knows that being idle is not for him. He has purpose and pleasure, and that is enough.

The story also offers a different perspective on subsistence living. Of course, accumulating wealth may protect you from the day when there are no fish to provide you with food, or the river becomes polluted, or you're too old to fish. In that regard, the fisherman would be making a sound economic decision to protect himself against the future if he accumulated the boats. But the fisherman values his life differently. For him, the experience of the moment is more valuable than the inevitabilities of the future. He recognizes that life's limits also mean that if we spend our lives always planning ahead and buying more stuff, we'll forget to actually live our lives and take pleasure in what we have.

By wanting more, are we therefore only setting ourselves up for disappointment? Ten years ago we may have thought we'd be living in a mansion and instead we're still living in an apartment. We thought we'd be driving a Mercedes, and yet we're still driving a Toyota. We thought we'd be the CEO of our company, and we look around us and we're still in middle management. Why do we have this relentless push to extend ourselves beyond what we need or would make us happy? Why don't we just stop and savor what we have?

Consider a friend of mine in Boston, Massachusetts, who had three jobs. When we got together, she always seemed tired and I told her once that I didn't think she should work so hard. "I know," she replied. "But I was able to buy a house with my jobs, and now I'd like to buy a second one."

"How long do you stay in your house every day?" I asked her.

She turned to me and, rather sadly I thought, said, "I just go back to sleep in it."

I was amazed. My friend never got a chance to sit down on the couch or decorate her house or enjoy the fruits of ownership. She was too busy working at her jobs, so she could accumulate more and more. Surely, accumulation is not where our happiness lies; it's in the enjoyment of the little we have where happiness resides. And we don't have to own things to take pleasure in them. We can enjoy nature.

Now of course being productive is a good thing, and work should not be shunned. We should feel busy and creative, accomplishing tasks and meeting deadlines. But we should go about it without being mentally anxious. Worrying about the unnecessary things—the factors that are out of our control or whether someone does or does not like us—will not only reduce the pleasure of our work, but probably make us less efficient and productive. Similarly, constantly fretting about the outcome of our labors will make us less likely to produce in such a way that the outcome of that labor will be a good one. In other words, we're being our own worst enemy, sabotaging our chance for happiness and success by worrying about whether we'll be happy or successful. If we insistently fear disappointment, then we cannot be surprised if we're often disappointed.

One way people medicate themselves against their disappointment or try to lessen the stress of living in a world where they're judged by what they have rather than who they are is to take drugs. Drugs in and of themselves aren't a problem. After all, we use many drugs to heal us, and many shamanic and other religious authorities throughout the long history of spirituality and healing have used mind-altering substances for the purposes of divination or to gain insight into the deep mysteries of life.

What *is* the problem is when the use of drugs is divorced from a regulated societal context and the ingestion or application of drugs becomes pathological. This involves not only proscribed drugs—such as heroin, cocaine, crystal methamphetamine, and alcohol beneath a certain age, etc. It also includes prescribed drugs—drugs that keep us calm or pep us up. This need to medicate ourselves with something, to dull our senses or make us able to work or play harder, or even to remain sexually active past our sexual peak, is part of a decontextualized world of seeking solutions to the symptom of the problem rather than delving into the cause. If we're feeling lethargic, then we need to understand the psychological reasons why we don't find life compelling; if we act with nervous anxiety and want to be calmed down, then we need to ask ourselves what it is about our lifestyles that makes us this way. Sometimes the answers are surprisingly simple: we're not sleeping enough, our jobs aren't fulfilling, we're having problems in our relationships, we're not eating the right foods. Solutions cannot always be found through medication; sometimes they require self-examination.

Even though drugs themselves are, therefore, not the ultimate problem, their misuse obviously has serious consequences. It's clearly wrong to be using drugs when we should be caring for our own health, looking after our family, or earning a living. We shouldn't have to steal money or goods in order to feed our drug habit. We shouldn't place ourselves at risk of giving ourselves HIV/AIDS through intravenous injections and we shouldn't place someone else at risk by sharing potentially infected needles. Buddhist ethics also teach us to recognize that cause and effect reach beyond one's immediate action. This is why we shouldn't sell drugs, even if the person buying drugs is a consenting adult; We don't know whether they are ruining other peoples' lives because of the habit we're helping to maintain. Furthermore, even if no one is directly hurt because we sell drugs, if the neighborhood is less safe for people to live and work in because of dealers and addicts coming in, then that's effectively bringing harm to others. And sometimes that cause and effect can reach even further. We need to consider who might have died for the drugs to be shipped to these shores, how many guns were bought with the money we paid, and how many died as a result of the bullets that were fired because of the drugs we thought only harmed us, and us alone.

Like other forms of junk (it's surely instructive that one of the names for heroin is *junk*), drugs can be momentarily intensely pleasurable. All one's cravings and satisfactions are, for a brief period of time, satisfied, and indeed our senses may be enhanced. Just like when we bring our big screen TV home and set it up and settle down with our remote control, taking drugs makes us feel *good*. But, with drugs, there can never be enough. The need for them changes the nature of the need by altering the chemical processes of the brain, so that the higher we get from the drugs, the more we need to satisfy that high. There can never be enough; and we can never stop ourselves once we begin to satisfy the craving. You cannot be a halfway addict, or "sort of" taking drugs. This is the nature of dependency. We shouldn't feel morally superior to the addict, either, for drug addicts are no more depraved or morally at sea than the rest of us. None of us is immune to the allure of intense, if momentary, satisfaction; who knows what particular addictions we all feed?

It should be understood, of course, that what is true for cocaine and heroin is also true for alcohol and tobacco. Most countries in the world sanction either one or both of these drugs, and some valorize them as statements of maturity, coolness, or pleasure. And it's hard to deny: a glass of wine can be very pleasurable, and smoking can reduce stress. But as we've seen in the last few decades, the costs of alcohol abuse and addiction to nicotine in terms of illness and premature death are very high. Alcohol in particular can lead to deeply destructive patterns of addiction. I've known generations of families that have been affected by the lies, violence, failures, and ultimately tragedy of the individual who's an alcoholic. Alcoholics Anonymous (AA) and other such groups have performed an invaluable service in forcing people to go deep into the processes of addiction to understand what it is that made them give up everything that was dear and important to them so they could feed their addiction. Although many of these organizations place a primacy on surrendering to God, as a Buddhist I can see how profoundly "Buddhist" is the concept of being honest with ourselves and tearing away the veils of deception that we've used to cover up our lies. In forcing us to confront the reality of our pain and our loneliness, AA and Buddhism can work hand in hand to enable the addict to build a self that is honest, has integrity, and is able to confront its demons with strength and conviction.

Pleasure is an important feature of our lives. But when it becomes merely an attempt to get a chemical high by stimulating areas of the brain that produce serotonin, and when we need to consume more and more of that substance or become more promiscuous to feed our addiction, then what

was natural is perverted. Essentially what is missing is consciousness: of being in control of the mind and its thoughts.

In fact, it's instructive that the precept against taking intoxicants in Buddhism is considered slightly different from
the other four precepts (not to kill, not to steal, not to lie,
and not to practice sexual misconduct). I think most of us
would agree that the first four precepts are wrong under any
moral system. However, the fifth precept is debatable, since
ostensibly no one is directly harmed by the transgression. Indeed, in some contexts the Buddha agreed that it was not
breaking any rules to give wine to someone who was sick,
since the wine would act medicinally.

The Buddha in a story in a sutra explains the reason for
the prohibition of alcohol: A man feels the need for a drink,
and then once he has become drunk he feels the need for
some food. So he goes out and spots a chicken in his neighbor's backyard, steals it, and then kills the bird. When the
neighbor finds her chicken is missing, she goes to the man
and asks him whether he saw the bird. "No," says the man,
and begins to harass the woman sexually. In a short period of
time, illustrates the story, the man has broken four precepts
because he's intoxicated. When I tell my students this story
they think it isn't relevant to their lives. However, I also remind them of people who, their behavioral restraints loos-
ened by drink at a party, have had inappropriate sexual
contact and have woken up the next morning not knowing
what they've done or with whom. They may have been raped

or end up pregnant. This can lead to an abortion or the young person lying to her parents, or maxing out her credit cards in order to pay for the termination, or killing or dumping her baby when it's born. In this way, the woman commits offenses against all four precepts because of her use of alcohol. These stories show Buddhism contextualizing misdeeds to provide an example of how immoderation in one part of our lives can lead to other acts of immoderation that build on one another.

One way of understanding addiction from a Buddhist perspective is from the Yogacara school of Mahayana Buddhism, which began in the fourth and fifth centuries of the Common Era. When we take alcohol, or partake of any other addictive substance or situation, a seed of experience is planted in our consciousness. While, as some contemporary science argues, we may be predisposed to addictive behavior by our genes, Buddhism suggests that the seed of that predisposition is only taken in by our action and then is watered and fed by our environment (in other words, in the case of alcoholism, whether we live with alcoholics, are constantly around alcohol, or believe that we need alcohol to relax or fit in, etc.). Every time we use our drug of choice, we're strengthening the conditions for the full flowering of what we might call the "addiction garden" by adding another seed: one cigarette, for instance, is one seed; a hundred cigarettes are a hundred seeds. In this way, we create the conditions for our own addiction, by nurturing what we've already planted and adding more and more seeds for the garden of personal destruction to grow.

Of course, there are people who are clinically depressed and for whom medication is the only option. Contemporary Western medicine is reconsidering addiction as a disease and we have to have compassion for those who are caught helplessly in the web of addiction that ensnares not only the addict, but the addict's family, friends, and the whole society that every day is paying for the addiction, whether in law enforcement, lost labor hours, and a host of other social pathologies. Sometimes there seems to be so much pain in people's souls, so much that they are scared of or wish to run away from, that not a single ray of light or hope can escape the great Black Hole of every individual addict's compulsive need to destroy him- or herself.

At least a part of the problem of addiction in the West has to do with the primacy that the West has put on individual freedom, divorced from social responsibility and the claims and benefits of the family. Because Buddhism believes that nothing that we think or do is without consequence, it places limits on the idea that an individual can do whatever they want without hurting someone else. It demands that we think more deeply about our actions and reflect on the possibility that what we do may not have either immediate or visible consequences—that, in fact, we may never know whom we've affected, or how much pain or suffering we've inflicted. It asks us to be extra cautious in our self-indulgence.

It also redefines what "freedom" might be. In the West, we consider freedom to be, first, the ability and right to do whatever we want to do, as long as it doesn't impinge on the rights of others to do what *they* want to do; and then, secondly, the freedom not to do those things we don't want to do. Buddhism has an additional freedom: the freedom from doing what we *want* to do! So much of what we take for freedom consists in fact of tired, pre-programmed compulsions that we actually gain little enjoyment or satisfaction from. Buddhism asks us to re-examine every part of our so-called "freedom" and imagine a pared-down world where we appreciate the freedom to be who we are and not whom others expect us to be; do the things that matter and not occupy our time with wasteful and pointless busyness; and work on the projects that bring joy and hope to others rather than grind through the day to accumulate stuff we never use.

Once, I visited a friend's house in Texas—a house so huge that I quite literally got lost in it. I asked him, "I hope you enjoy this house. Because you have to take care of the inside and keep an eye on the deck as well, and pay for all the upkeep." I couldn't imagine the burdens of protecting the property and maintaining all the services it provided. All I had to do was to sleep in the bedroom and enjoy the place for a few days. But he had to worry about it all the time. There's a Buddhist verse that says, "Even though I own thousands of acres of land, the place where I sleep is only six feet long." It's worth remembering that that length applies not only to your sleeping quarters but your grave as well.

So what should we do to deal with all the junk that we've accumulated or we may be addicted to? Every New Year, we all make resolutions: We're going to lose weight, or stop eating chocolate, or finally get around to writing that book we've been planning for years. However, when New Year comes around I always ask people to check their inventory—of both material and spiritual possessions. I ask them to reflect on what's necessary and what isn't, and to dispose of the garbage.

Of course, we don't have to wait until it's New Year to take out the trash. Why not do it now, and start again? We should check our inventory and give it away. Clean up our house and clean up our life. What should we dispense with? Well, there's an important distinction that we can make: What do we absolutely need and what do we only desire? If we look at what we have with such a distinction in mind, we'll be amazed at just how little we need to live with. Clearing out what we don't need will also, paradoxically, make us value what we keep that much more. It will enable us, quite literally, to see what we couldn't see before, since it was hidden behind or under the piles of other stuff, our delusions and illusions, which were blocking our view and denying us the opportunity to use what was truly valuable.

There is a facet of junk stuff that many people don't

think about when they worry about all the material possessions that fill their houses. They forget that much of that stuff
was in fact produced with no care at all. Women and children
working in terrible conditions for very little money in a
sweatshop somewhere in the world might have made their
T-shirts or socks or shoes. Perhaps their clothes were put together shoddily so that they fell apart only after a few hours'
or days' use. Or they might have been manufactured using
dangerous chemicals or toxins that not only harmed the
workers, and the animals on which the products were tested,
but polluted the land where the workers lived, and could
even harm them, the purchasers.

There are other aspects of junk stuff that we should
think about. The first is the wrapping that the stuff comes in.
It's rare that we buy anything in a box these days without
having to deal with the plastic, paper, bubble wrap, and polystyrene packing peanuts that products come swathed in.
Sometimes it seems impossible actually to measure the utility
or worth of a product because all we can really see is the
packaging and the wrapping. And these pieces of packaging
are not harmless. The plastic rings that hold the six-packs of
beer in place have ended up in the stomachs of animals or
wrapped around the beaks of birds. The thin plastic bags that
are used throughout the developing world, and which often
break after one usage, end up in trees and bushes, or at the
roadside, where they allow water to pool and provide a
breeding ground for mosquitoes. And then there are the Sty-

rofoam cups that crumble in our hands after use, and the plastic utensils that we toss in the trash can along with those little plastic containers for sauce. What about the wooden chopsticks that we use once and get thrown away, and which may have come from a rainforest? Was it worthwhile using them when we could have asked for a metal fork that could be washed and used again?

Let's ask ourselves when we next go into a supermarket: Do we really need the one or two items we purchased to be in a plastic bag rather than a paper sack? And why not bring a canvas or string bag next time? What would happen, do you think, if instead of being asked by the cashier whether we *wanted* a plastic bag, we were asked whether we *needed* one? What if we were given money back if we *didn't* use a plastic bag?

Some supermarkets and other vendors are now instituting such programs, and this is a welcome change. My own temple, the Hsi Lai temple in Hacienda Heights, California, once used polystyrene plates and cups in its dining room, but it's now using washable and reusable plastic plates and utensils instead. In his book *Living Affinity*, Venerable Master Hsing Yun talks eloquently of the importance of not wasting resources and making conservation part of our everyday life. But it's sad that we don't take more of the initiative ourselves. Many of us had parents or grandparents who belonged to the generations that grew up during a war or lived in an economic depression. They couldn't afford *not* to conserve resources and practice thrift. Many people from that time look at today's world and see only waste and extravagance. They cannot believe how much food we throw away. Likewise, they remember the few possessions they had with great affection. In our recognition that the Earth's natural resources are under threat, we're belatedly rediscovering this wisdom of care and thrift, which today is known as conservation but which once came naturally to people who were accustomed to being meticulous with what they owned.

In some ways, our attitude toward stuff depends on the culture we grow up in and the values taught to us by our parents. When I was a child in Taiwan during the 1960s and 1970s, my mother taught me how to save money before she educated me on how to make it. I'm always teasing that Asian parents never teach their kids how to spend money even after they make it. I think that that's a very typical Eastern attitude to money. Having lived in the West now for a number of years, I see a very different mentality. In the West, a child is taught from a very early age how to spend money, even before they make it. And they're never taught how to save money after they begin to earn it. Economically, of course, there are pros and cons to both approaches. Japan's economy in the 1990s was stagnant because people were saving money and not spending it. The United States has an enormous trade deficit partly because Americans love to buy things, although those things tend to be made outside the United States. But, economics alone cannot satisfy human needs; nor can it justify another aspect of junk products, about which I'll talk next.

Junk products are not just throwaway trinkets or poorly made disposable or novelty items, made of cheap plastic or other man-made chemicals. Nor are they only products made in sweatshops by women and children over long hours and for very little money. Junk products are also diamonds that have been mined from areas where rebel and corrupt government forces use them to buy weapons that kill civilians or dragoon children into militias. They're chocolates that have been created using cocoa from countries where children are forced into slave labor to harvest the beans. They come from slaughterhouses where the speed at which the animals are processed is so fast that the workers are often severely injured and are forced to kill the animals without due regard to the pain or suffering of either worker or animal. Junk products are those that strip the Earth of her precious resources for temporary satisfaction or our convenience—such as columbite-tantalite (more commonly known as coltan), a component of capacitors in cell phones and other electronic devices, and the extraction of which has fuelled environmental destruction, the displacement of peoples, and conflict in the war-torn Democratic Republic of Congo.

As these last examples bear witness to, what we decide to buy, and from whom, have consequences. There are also consequences in what we choose to throw away. Whole industries depend on our disposal of things, and throughout the cities of the developing world you can see adults and children digging through the mountains of trash shipped to them from the industrialized world, scrabbling for anything they can use or sell. But we shouldn't be happy about this particular form of recycling. The enormous mounds of waste are often full of chemicals and poisons that are in various processes of disintegration or decomposition. They are inherently unstable piles that can shift without notice, replete with noxious gases that can explode into flame, or a mass of sharp edges that can cut the skin and infect those who venture onto the huge heaps of junk. This junk might be electronic waste (old cell phones, broken or unfashionably out-of-date computers and monitors, cables and wires, capacitors and keyboards) dumped in Africa or China. It might be huge tankers beached and rusting on the shores of the Bay of Bengal, being torn apart piece by piece by men who risk life and limb to salvage the metals and the refuse. It might be the ten thousand bits of debris, from defunct satellites to old nuts and bolts and empty rockets, that are orbiting Earth— testimony to the fact that we're no longer content to despoil our planet but are now littering space. It's the nuclear and toxic waste that will last tens of thousands of years and can end up on the high seas, shipped from this place to the next, a cargo wanted in no port, the result of our incessant demand for energy so we can consume more and more.

Every time I bring my trash to the dump, I feel relieved to have gotten rid of it. However, I also reflect that I'm only one person, and that I've created all this trash. And then I think: If everyone created the same or more trash as mine, then what a gigantic mountain of trash that would make! Finally, I remember Mother Earth: How much of a burden she has to bear because of the profligacy of her human children! How can she swallow it all, or how will she keep the sweetness of her breath when she has to inhale all those fumes from all those incinerators? But I still make trash, and I still tend to throw it out thoughtlessly. You may have been walking along the street and seen someone take the wrapper from a box of cigarettes and throw it on the ground, and you wonder how someone could be so thoughtless. But their response and yours is actually the same: someone else will clean it up. It's someone else's problem.

When we can't recycle our trash on site, we ship it elsewhere, bury it in the ground, or burn it. But, in a perfect example of Buddhist ecology, the junk doesn't disappear. It merely breaks down (sometimes very, very slowly) into its constituent parts and returns karmically to us in the form of acid rain, polluted rivers, dead oceans, and barren landscapes. It also, as we've seen, makes some societies unstable, as we unload our unwanted material, weaponry, and illnesses on them; and their citizens ultimately demand our attention when our conscience has been sufficiently pricked or they arrive in vast numbers on our borders demanding entry. The cycle continues: the more stuff we produce, the more there is to throw away, and the more unsteady the world becomes as the room to put it in shrinks. If we're having problems organizing the stuff in our houses, how do we expect to be able to organize the stuff on our planet? And if our response is to be overwhelmed, why should we not expect that the planet's ecosystems themselves will be overwhelmed?

Ultimately, we're going to be forced to respond to our constant desire for junk and our failure to use it wisely by employing the wisdom of the planet. Nowhere in the universe, so far as we know, is there a more creative or promiscuous manufacturer, or more efficient and ruthless recycler, than planet Earth. Every day it takes the raw materials gathered from the sun and generates and regenerates everything on it, including human beings. And every day it breaks down, decomposes, rots, and reuses those elements in mammoth cycles of which we still only understand a tiny part. In all of the profligacy that is the planet's biotic system, nothing is wasted; there is no junk. Everything eventually turns into something else.

In spite of our relatively new arrival and infinitesimally short time on this planet, in a matter of a little over two hundred years *Homo sapiens* has managed to place this extraordinary, mysterious system under enormous strain. If we continue on our current course of consuming much more than we're renewing we will threaten the survival of tens of thousands of species. While Earth will most likely survive and regenerate itself in the way that it's done throughout the course of its existence, the upheavals and suffering that our reckless activities will cause will be monumental. In the popular imagination and in our language, we consider the dinosaurs to be symbols of failure, a species that outlived its capacity and couldn't adapt to changing climates. Yet these creatures survived hundreds of millions of years. We've been around about two hundred thousand years in our current form, and within a few hundred more we may even render ourselves extinct.

I like to think that we'll stop before it's too late, that we'll manufacture products that degrade completely or can be used over and over again without any diminution of their utility or destruction of the planet on which we all depend. I like to believe that we'll start honoring the ecological systems by copying their wisdom rather than working against them. I hope that we'll learn that using what we *need* rather than simply *desire* is not just a virtue reserved for monastics or ascetics, but a decision that will help us value the simple fact that, unlike the tens of thousands of planets that we know about, our planet actually *supports* life (at least for a few billion years more) and wants it to continue. And I pray that we'll all honor our planet's sacred rhythms rather than asserting control through extracting, stripping, and cutting down everything in our madcap rush to get more and more junk. We owe it to our Mother.

3 ✻ Communication

Have you had this experience? You go to your front door to collect what the mail carrier has delivered. Among the ever present bills or magazines that you subscribe to, or even that rare letter or gift sent to you by a friend or family member, are a whole host of unsolicited catalogs, fundraising appeals, flyers, postcards, and other direct mail that's been pushed through your door in the hope that you'll buy whatever they are trying to sell. You dutifully put the unopened envelopes in the recycling bag and take it to the curb once a week. This bag is picked up by the garbage trucks and taken to the recycling center where energy is used to sort it and turn it into tissue or toilet paper and sent around the world.

Or perhaps you recognize this situation? You turn on your computer and check your email. There, in spite of the best filters, your inbox is filled with email "spam": advertise-

49

ments for drugs to enhance your sex life, exciting offers to help you with your heart condition or hair loss, suggestions you buy this stock or that share, or various schemes and other fraudulent activities that entice you to part with your money. You visit a website and up pop numerous boxes with advertisements that the site sells so it can make money. You turn on the television, and no matter what station you visit there are advertisements before, during, and after the programs. Sometimes it's hard to tell the program from the advertisements; while the half-hour nightly news show on network television in the U.S. has almost the same amount of advertisements, or "messages," in thirty minutes as it has news.

Or maybe this scenario is familiar? The telephone rings and you pick it up and there's somebody on the phone soliciting something from, or trying to sell something to, you. Sometimes it's not even a person, just a recorded message. Sometimes the person may shout obscenities down the line at you or it may be a sexual predator breathing heavily (something that happens to a surprising number of women). So you screen your calls or use an answering machine or caller ID to check on who is calling. Faxes appear from companies offering cruises or special bargains. You call the toll-free number to get yourself removed from the automatic fax list, but they still keep on coming.

This is some of the junk communication of our daily life, and we've allowed ourselves to be taken over by it. We may have tried valiantly to remove ourselves from the mailing lists to which the magazines we subscribe to sold our name, even when we asked them not to give our address to another company. We invested in spam blockers and pop-up advertisement filters and changed our email address to get away from the junk messages, or spam, which ironically was named after junk meat. We tried to cut ourselves off as much as we could from the cacophony of advertisements by not watching network television or only listening to public radio, but everywhere we turn information is being "sponsored" or "brought to" us or "underwritten" by somebody else.

Naturally, of course, we all understand that people need to be told about products or events, and that advertising is an important way that people get their messages out to those who might support them. The Internet has also offered people a chance to pursue their enthusiasms and find community all over the world, as well as provided access to seemingly limitless funds of the world's knowledge at the click of a computer mouse. However, in this exponential increase in the amount of information we are exposed to, we're in danger of becoming overloaded. Everything around us seems to be so loud and unrelenting. The more we are sold to, the more we try to tune it out, which means that advertising must become more intrusive and flashier in order to make itself heard or seen. And this vicious cycle continues, with everything getting more intense and more pervasive.

It's true that advertising and freedom of speech and expression are functions of living in an open society. However, sometimes that freedom can drive people to the edge of sanity so cacophonous and demanding is the sound of people demanding to be heard. I also believe that there's an element of violence in some of those claims to free expression. Some rap and hip hop music, as well as some rock and roll and other extreme music and lyrics, contain violent and misogynistic words that cannot but plant the seeds of violence in those who listen to them. At the very least, they assault the ears and cultivate a lack of respect. I believe these sounds pollute art and challenge what freedom of speech means. Whose freedom is being expressed and whose is being compromised when violent and offensive words are thrown into the air from passing cars and boom boxes or radio stations and cable television and channeled directly into the ears of impressionable young men and women? What about being free from cultural norms that demand we sit back passively and compliantly and be told that women are bitches and whores, that glamour comes through shooting someone or breaking the law, and that mindless sex and material accumulation are the point of life? Sometimes we confuse our freedoms, and the more we claim our right to liberty, the more we enchain ourselves to the things that will ultimately never satisfy us.

The constant bombardment of such unsolicited mail and advertisements, however, is not the only way that we are exposed to junk messages. There's also the way we communicate. How many unnecessary emails or text messages do we send? How many thoughtless comments, frivolous or throwaway observations, or snide remarks do we throw out? How much of our day do we spend gossiping idly or maliciously about other people? Gossip is rarely just gossip. It contains deeper distractions and more insidious tendencies. As Venerable Master Hsing Yun says: "Not worrying about trifles lets you unload your mental burden. Not listening to gossip lets you avoid disputes." Gossip—superficial and unfounded—also says something about us as people. As a Chinese proverb has it: "Deep water flows quietly and a shallow creek flows noisily."

We should take the time to ask ourselves these questions: How often do we flatter someone or over-dramatize a situation to gain a temporary advantage? How much of the time do we waste words in cursing someone or something out, or thinking malign or prejudiced thoughts? How much effort do we exert lying or speaking out of the sides of our mouths; how much do we bend the truth or manipulate the facts to suit our needs or get ourselves out of events or relationships we'd rather not confront honestly or directly? How many hours per week do we spend reading tabloids about celebrity lives and worrying about whether they're getting married or divorced, or what hairstyles or clothes or houses they're acquiring? Why should we be so interested in invading their privacy when we'd be mortified if our lives were held up to public scrutiny in the same way? How much television do we watch or how many websites do we visit that neither genuinely entertain nor inform us? And how often do we use the same merely to anesthetize ourselves from dealing with the realities of our lives?

Even in an area where our communication should be most tender and most careful—the communication with our loved ones—we often fall short. You probably know of someone who's always complaining about their partner rather than talking to them directly. How many rows have escalated into verbal abuse and shouting matches before ending up with somebody hitting somebody else or storming out and slamming the door? If either party had only minded their language, then perhaps things wouldn't have reached such a terrible stage.

A story was sent to me the other day, which while funny has a more serious message underneath. A husband and wife were having a fight and, as the tempers increased and the insults flew, the couple finally reached such a fever pitch that they resolved never to speak with each other again. Furiously, the husband wrote a message on a piece of paper and handed it to his wife: "Wake me up at five a.m. I have a plane to catch." The next day, the husband woke up and looked at his watch. It was nine o'clock and he'd missed his flight. He turned and found his wife had gone out and next to him in bed was a message, written on another piece of paper in her hand. "Wake up," it said. "It's five a.m." Now do you see why it's important to speak to each other?!

I've observed that when couples fight, they use the same

language over and over again, repeating what was said in the past and using offensive language in a vicious cycle where nothing is actually communicated except insult and ridicule. It's as if neither partner actually wishes to get through to the other; they only want to communicate their own pain and humiliation and make their loved one feel what they're experiencing. How does either party expect anything to improve if neither is willing to hear what the other is saying or communicate effectively what they want to change? Mostly, of course, when we reach such a stage, what's mainly hurt is our pride: our egos have been bruised and we don't see why we should back down. And yet we gain no benefit from our pride; we still feel rotten, even if we still have the perverse satisfaction of not climbing down and admitting that we were at least partially to blame. I'll talk more about communication in the chapter on junk thoughts and emotions.

Sometimes the problem is that we don't communicate with each other at all. I vividly recall visiting the home of a devotee of Fo Guang Shan. The devotee had a son, and a friend of hers had brought her own son to visit so that the children could play together and build a friendship. When I went to talk to the kids, I found them sitting side by side in front of two computers, typing on keyboards, and their eyes focused on the screen. It's true that they were talking to each other—but they were doing it through an online chat room, even though at that moment they were sitting next to each other in the same room! That struck me as the height of absurdity, as well as tragic. All they had to do was to turn to face each other and talk. But they couldn't imagine "interfacing" except through the computer.

I also recall the children of our devotees who come to the temple on a regular basis. While their parents are carrying out their rituals, the children will occupy themselves by lying down on a couch and playing video games. Most of these games involve shooting and killing, loud music and aggression. I remind the parents not to let their children allow violent seeds to be planted in their minds, but some of them shrug their shoulders and tell me that they cannot stop their children from playing these games because the kids experience "peer pressure" and would feel left out if they didn't do or have what everyone else has. Here the vital communication between parents and their children is broken. The child doesn't speak to his or her father or mother but is glued to a video game, and a parent feels they cannot guide their child appropriately because they worry about their child's social standing.

I saw a segment on the American television program *60 Minutes*, which aired on July 23, 2006, in which the reporter Leslie Stahl asked why Americans were working longer and not demanding more pay. The answer was because of the ubiquity of wireless Internet access, handheld devices, cell phones, and electronic personal organizers. All these items made people contactable at any time, anywhere in the world. This meant that, unless you were careful, you'd never have any respite from the demands of your job. You'd be on call no matter where you were or what time of day it was. You might not be physically in your office, but you were never not at work.

Leslie Stahl profiled some high achieving people who seemed to have no problem with the lifestyle that these devices were enabling them to pursue. Some were getting up in the middle of the night to send emails, or driving on six-lane highways while typing in messages through their electronic personal organizers, which I thought was dangerous not only to them but to the drivers around them. A couple text-messaged each other even though they were sitting in the same house, only a room away from each other; and a man had a television in his shower so he wouldn't have to miss a moment of information while he was soaping himself down. Leslie Stahl was astonished at such a life, and so was I. What was so essential that these individuals couldn't take a few more moments to sleep or shower or concentrate on the road? What happened to working to live rather than living to work? What happened to getting up and talking to someone?

It makes me sad when I think about those of us who never find the time to talk to each other. And by "talk to" I don't mean the kind of distracted sharing of information or scheduling that passes for talk these days. Nor do I mean the trafficking in gossip or innuendo and frivolities that fill our airwaves or water cooler conversations. And nor do I mean the use of email to confront and act aggressively toward people whom we can't, or won't, talk to face to face. I mean honest listening and attentiveness.

I'll talk about this shortly. But first, I want to reflect for a moment on a kind of junk conversation where we're being what the German philosopher Martin Heidegger (1889–1976) called *das Man*. *Das Man* is the everyday and impersonal public face of who we are. It's the type of individual who doesn't mean what he says, and who doesn't bother whether he's authentic or truthful. He gets by on white lies, exaggerations, small talk, and sarcasm. In the process, the individual forgets who he is and replaces his authentic self with a kind of shallow and flexible persona that adapts to all things and believes in nothing.

We all have a little of *das Man* in us. We spend so much of our time wondering what other people are thinking or saying about us: Do they find us interesting, or desirable, or estimable, or likeable? This is also junk communication, for we're actually not communicating anything to anyone. Indeed, we may not actually want to have the answers to such questions! Instead, to reflect on Heidegger's ideas, we're "throwing ourselves forward" at each moment in time, speculating on how we might be perceived by others. This means that we never actually live in the moment or give ourselves a chance for genuine insight into who we are and what our place is in the world. As we'll see, Buddhism also has insight into this kind of junk consciousness.

The result of this self-forgetfulness (Selbstvergessenheit), to use one of Heidegger's words, is a profound alienation from the world and other human beings. We no longer know who we are; we're only the collection of other people's impressions of us, and our impressions of their impressions. Our advanced capitalist society has built upon that self-forgetfulness to create economic and social compartments where we can be measured, analyzed, sold to, or rated. We're consumers and not citizens; demographic and economic units rather than individuals; laborers, line-managers, supervisors, and workers rather than artisans and creators; Soccer Moms, Nascar Dads, values voters, liberal elites, and so on, rather than…human beings.

While we've willingly submitted ourselves to junk communication, we also embrace it very actively ourselves. You've undoubtedly heard of the schoolyard taunt: "Sticks and stones may break my bones, but words will never hurt me." Well, is that really true? Words can be sharper than a sword; for whereas a physical wound can be healed with time and a bandage, a harsh word, or constant criticism, can be carried by the victim for a whole life—leaving her debilitated and full of self-doubt. As Venerable Master Hsing Yun says: "A kind word brings warmth in the chill of winter, while a harsh word burns more than summer's heat."

Given the bombardment of images and words coming back at us from the various media that surround us and the cacophony of people trying to get our attention, the most subversive and self-protective thing we can do is actually the simplest, even if it is paradoxical: to tune out the noise and to listen to those who truly need to be heard. To listen means to genuinely pay attention to what someone is saying to us. It means sitting down with a friend or an acquaintance and attending respectfully and generously to their words and following the expression on their face. It means turning off the cell phone or beeper, unplugging ourselves from our portable listening device, or switching off our personal organizer, and entering into the world of the person sitting opposite from us and, without distraction or impatience, genuinely taking note of what they're saying. It means asking questions and honestly wanting to know someone's opinion. It's an irony that one of the only times that some people feel they're being actually listened to is when they visit their therapists. It's a sad commentary on our supposedly advanced societies that we have to give money to people so they'll listen to us. Conversely, what can we say about genuine conversation when listening properly is a task for professionals?

These are relatively simple tasks, when we think about it. And yet they seem increasingly hard to do. Often as not, families these days don't sit down at dinner together or at all. If they do, they're watching television, in silence. When they do get around to talking, they might speak, as it were, past each other, interrupting and second-guessing, cutting each other off in mid-sentence. They may hear what their conversational partners say, but they don't listen. They may respond, but not to delve more deeply into what someone has said, but to try to top it with an anecdote of their own. They're talking *at* and not *with* each other. It sometimes feels to me that the electronic media have now perfected this art of filling the world with people who speak like this. There are pundits, bloggers, experts, and spokespeople everywhere we turn. They rant, pontificate, shout, belittle, ridicule, protest, defame, and bloviate about everything and nothing, filling our ears with empty invective until all we want to do is to put our hands to our face and, like the famous painting by Norwegian artist Edvard Munch, scream.

Amidst all of the sound and fury that signifies, as Shakespeare's Macbeth knows, nothing, we've forgotten the greatest communicative gift of all: silence. This world is so full of chatter, of hawkers and salespeople and consultants and advertisers and pitchers and spinners, that we've forgotten that if we and they would just shut up we might be able to hear the quietest and yet most important interlocutor that we'll ever know: our inner voice. That voice is the one that expresses our deepest needs and hopes. It's the articulator of our truest self. Perhaps it's because we don't want to know what it will say to us that we drown it out with all manner of noise.

There is a Chinese expression that artfully captures the different kinds of ways someone who is incompetent speaks. At the beginning, the person promises the world using deceiving words. After this they use enthusiastic words. When they are unable to deliver, the incompetent person uses in-consistent words, and when they are finally shown to be use-less, they say nothing. While I was writing this chapter, a friend sent me an email, which had as part of it, a piece in Chinese called "The Temperature of Speech." This was the thrust of the message, which I think carries a lot of wisdom about proper communication:

If something is urgent, say it slowly.

If something is important, say it clearly.

If something is unimportant, say it humorously.

If something is uncertain, say it discreetly.

If something did not happen, do not mention it at all.

If you cannot do something, do not claim it for yourself.

If what you say could harm others, keep silent.

When something annoys you, don't take it personally.

If something makes you happy, don't make too much of it.

When talking about your own affairs, pay attention to how you talk.

When talking about someone else's affairs, be judicious.

When your heart is broken, not everyone needs to know.

Of things that remain to be done, talk of them when they are finished.

Of things that happen in the future, don't talk of them in the present.

If I have not satisfied you, tell me.

The art of meditation is a wonderful way to still the

chatter and hear what the inner voice has to say to us. Meditation is, in fact, not that much of a mystery. The essence of meditation can be described as listening to our breath. If we're unable to concentrate, or stop the thoughts about our life, career, and relationships filling our head and distracting us from the process of calming the mind, then we should focus on the breath—the simple intake and expiration of breath—without which none of us would be alive and yet which we waste in the hot air that comes out of our mouth. Even after almost thirty years of being a nun, the fact of sitting down and following my breath still fills me with peace and joy.

The task of Buddhist meditation is to unpeel the layers of self, much as one would do an onion, to get to the heart of the self, which according to Buddhist philosophy, is no heart at all, but a recognition of the contingency of all things. The Buddha taught two kinds of meditation. One was called *samatha*, which basically means concentration or tranquility in meditation. The other was *vipassana*, which one would translate these days as insight meditation.

The process of meditation involves, to use familiar metaphors, the cleaning of the mirror or the stilling of the waters on a lake. We need to be still—and not only in our body, but also and essentially, in our mind. In *samatha* meditation, we start with the observation of our body and its inherent impurities, by which I mean the recognition of its contingencies and lack of permanence. We look at the impermanence of our mind and what passes through it and come to an understanding of the sensation of suffering. Sometimes we can focus on certain objects, like a statue of the Buddha or a candle, to help us in our concentration. Once the mind is clear or still, the point of Buddhist meditation is not to stay there, but to move beyond the mirror or the still lake to see the true reflection and analyze all the phenomena of this world. This is the task of insight meditation. Insight meditation attempts to understand the interdependent origination of all things, and through this grasp the essence of the dharma, or the truth.

Let us explore this metaphor in greater depth. Our mind is like a lake full of muddy water. Our emotions blow across the disturbed water so that it's impossible either to see through it to the bottom of the lake or, because the waves are disturbed, to see an accurate reflection off the surface. What meditation does is reduce the turbulence until there is no more disturbance on the surface. At that point, the reflection on the water becomes clearer. However, this is only part of the process, because although the reflection off the water is now undisturbed, the water is still muddy, and thus, for instance, the sun looks a dull brown color rather than the bright yellow light that it is. We need to do more.

As the water is stilled, however, something else happens. This is the gift of *vipassana* meditation. The mud begins to settle and sink to the bottom, leaving the water clear and clean. Now that the water is clear as well as still, we are not only able to see a true reflection, but we get the proper colors. The water's transparency also allows us to see into the depths and ascertain a truer sense of the dimensions of the lake. *Vipassana* meditation also draws upon the Daoist philosophy of non-action (*wu-wei*), whereby we are involved as one with the medium that we perceive. When the mirror is so clear that there's not the tiniest amount of distortion, it reflects spontaneously and accurately our surroundings. During *vipassana* meditation, the calm mind reflects the environment as it is.

Hopefully, the metaphor is self-explanatory. The mud consists of our thoughts while the turbulence consists of how we react to these thoughts. We first need to stop reacting and thinking these thoughts and stirring up our soul. Then we need to let the thoughts clear by having them settle to the bottom of our consciousness and let the clarity of mind that is the water emerge. At that moment, we'll be able to see more clearly into the nature of things and direct our attention to the nature of reality. Note that the practice of meditation is not the end point of our quest—for the task is to provide an accurate *reflection* of reality. Furthermore, just as water refracts light slightly and even the clearest water can disguise the true depth of a lake, meditation is merely one of the means by which we work over many lifetimes to approach the real—the point where formal apperception vanishes and a full realization of the inherent emptiness of all things is attained.

Many people in the West assume that meditation is only a technique to calm us down and remove our stress and make us feel more relaxed. While meditation does indeed serve this function by stilling our minds, lowering our heartbeats, and helping us focus our breath, such psychosomatic results are neither the main nor the end purpose of meditation. The reason we need to calm the mind and focus the breath is to enable us, the meditator, to see more clearly the nature of reality and uncover the patterns and pathologies that have clouded our souls. In other words, the point of meditation is not to escape from life, but to confront it that much more openly and directly.

According to the Chinese Tiantai school of Buddhism, meditation should operate on three levels. The first level is a **meditation on emptiness**, whereby we empty ourselves of prejudice and preconceptions. The second level involves us attempting to understand our **conventional and provisional** existence and to take responsibility for all of our actions. Finally, the third level is the contemplation of the **Middle Path**. This is why Buddhist meditation is a discipline and not an indulgence; a practice and not an analgesic. It's not meant to make us feel better; it's intended to make us experience more immediately what has been dulled and denied, and through that experience to place it in proper perspective and, ultimately, gain enlightenment.

Like all practices, meditation takes, well, practice. We get better at it, and its rewards grow. At first we master the basics, and then the techniques deepen. We learn to relax the mind and train it at the same time. We learn to analyze our emotions and thoughts with equanimity and judge them as fairly as possible. Many people have stereotyped notions of what it means to meditate. They think that you need to sit for hours in an uncomfortable position—that meditation is about pain and self-denial. But meditation is not *about* anything. It's a technique for stilling the mind and developing the right tools for discernment.

Therefore, if we're sitting, we should be aware of whether we're sitting upright or relaxed, and make sure we're comfortable, but not so comfortable that we fall asleep. We should do an inventory of our body to make sure it is relaxed and upright: Are we frowning? Is our jaw tense? The idea is to keep the mind alert but not agitated, relaxed but not fuzzy or drowsy. The most well-known position for meditation—the lotus—is intended to allow the body to unwind and yet keep the posture uptight. However, it is not the only way to meditate; there is walking meditation and standing meditation, for instance.

Once we're sitting comfortably, we should first conduct an inventory of our senses. Is there numbness or soreness in any part of the body: in our legs or in our neck? Perhaps those feelings may not be unpleasant, but sometimes they may be. Secondly, we observe those feelings and experience them, but we shouldn't worry about them. Thirdly, we become aware of our emotions. Do we feel happy or unhappy?

Do we feel anxious or depressed? In the process of meditation, disturbing thoughts and pain may arise. This is a natural
result of becoming still. In such times, whether it's physical or
emotional discomfort, we place our consciousness and loving
attention at the place where the pain is, and breathe. We don't
deny the painful feelings or try to stop them; we simply focus
on them and be present to them. Often we'll find that we're
no longer able to locate the pain. We'll think it's in one place,
and then discover that it's somewhere else, and then somewhere else again, and soon we'll not be able to pinpoint the
pain at all.

Fourthly, we become aware of our psychological condition. Here we have gone beneath the temporary emotions
to the deeper substrate of our personality. At this point we'll
be aware of our character, its tendencies and ways of thinking
and feeling about things. Finally, we move to the level of consciousness, where we dig up the very deepest behavioral
"seeds" that are planted there and cause us to do certain
things. This is a crucial point. Buddhism understands that
we're always going to face distractions and events that knock
us off our path to an authentic life, and an ability to understand our motivations might, as the following Buddhist story
illustrates, be the difference between life and death.

Jing Pifeng was known as a very deep meditator; when
he entered meditation no one and nothing could disturb him.
One day, however, Yama (or Yan Luo in Chinese), the god of
the dead, sent a messenger in the form of a sprite to come

and collect Jing, since his time was up. When the sprite arrived where Jing Pifeng lived, he was unable to collect the adept's spirit since we cannot be taken to the dead unless our souls can be reached, and Jing's was beyond even death's hand because he was in such deep meditation.

Disappointed, the sprite asked people who knew Jing how he could awake Jing from his meditation. They told him that Jing was never out of sight of his begging bowl and that, if the sprite removed the bowl, Jing would leave his meditative state and the sprite would be able to have access to his consciousness. The sprite was pleased to hear this and so crept up on Jing and took away the bowl. Sure enough, Jing immediately came out of his meditative state.

"Where's my begging bowl?" he asked.

"Aha!" said the sprite. "I've caught you. I'm a messenger from Yama and you must now accompany me to the underworld."

At this Jing began to laugh. "For all these years," he said to the sprite, "I've wondered what it is that's holding me back from going even deeper into my consciousness through meditation. What I hadn't realized until now was that the begging bowl was my attachment, and that I could not meditate more deeply because of my attachment to it. You might as well take an iron chain and try to lasso the sky before you catch me." And with that, Jing let go of the bowl and re-entered meditation, thwarting the sprite, and Yama, yet again.

In many ways, to return to the theme of junk communication, the dynamic of meditation is a conversation, where
we're the listener and our thoughts are the speaker. We're not
trying to interrupt or deny what our thoughts are trying to
tell us. Instead, we're making a profound commitment to understand exactly what they're saying to us and through that
attention to perceive their basis in reality.

The drum that we use in the chanting program at Fo
Guang Shan provides an example of what I mean. The
Woodenfish Program is a month-long course that we hold
every year in Taiwan for college students interested in Buddhism (www.woodenfish.org). The program is named after a
drum that's shaped like the head of a fish and is used both as
a musical instrument and an aid to chanting. During chanting
meditation practice, the drum is beaten rhythmically to estab-
lish a tempo so meditators can chant in unison. The beat and
the chanting bring poise to the mind. Why is the drum in the
shape of a fish? The answer is because fish don't have eyelids,
and thus their eyes always remain open, even when they're
asleep. In Buddhism, this symbolizes to the person who's cultivating mindfulness that he or she needs to be always awake,
present, and aware—even when they're unconscious!

As we go deeper into the meditative process, we begin
to realize the inherent emptiness of existence and the imper-
manent nature of the self. We start to apprehend how everything is contingent on everything else. A simple analogy will
suffice to explain. Everyone knows what a car is. But if we re-

moved the tires, the seating, the engine, doors, transmission, chassis, roof, hubcaps, windows, lights, fender, and license plate, could the car still be said to exist? No, of course not. Likewise, everything that we take to be permanent is in fact a function of the relation of parts to each other—parts that are themselves made up of other parts that also work in relation to each other.

Some might see the Buddhist experience of the interdependence and the impermanence of all things as a sign that we are indeed only the composite of other people's impressions; that since there's no self to begin with we have no inherent authenticity. But this is to misunderstand and trivialize the nature of the meditative quest, just as assuming that the body isn't worth preserving because it will one day die is facile and counterproductive. As individuals, we're so mired in delusions about who we are and have acquired so many levels of what the Trappist monk Thomas Keating calls "false selves," that it is only the most enlightened souls who achieve insight into the non-self and the contingency of all things. When these great people have gained such an enlightened state, their response has not been to brush off existence as mere nothingness, or the suffering of all beings as simply contingency in action. Instead, they have experienced a compassion for all sentient beings so infinite and strong that they've refused the ultimate destination, which is to remove themselves from the cycle of birth, death, and rebirth, and have resolved to set themselves the impossible task of helping all sentient beings achieve enlightenment before them.

These are the *bodhisattvas*, and it is their example of deep care and concern that we should emulate. For the *bodhisattvas*, the reality of the experience of all beings speaks to them at the deepest level. It's as if they're engaged in the fullest, most meaningful conversations with all creation. For the rest of us, the daily practice of meditation allows us to peel back a few layers of untruth and try to live a little more authentically and honestly with ourselves and other people. It gives us a moment in the day when we quieten our own and other voices and find out who we really are. Meditation is extremely valuable in dealing with the junk thoughts and emotions that I talk about in a later chapter.

We may not be bodhisattvas, but in the daily round of meditation, however, we're nevertheless engaged with some profound Buddhist ideas. The Buddhist concept of reincarnation is framed as a cycle of birth, death, and rebirth that it calls *samsara*. But samsara isn't, I believe, simply confined to the beginning and end of our lives. In fact, we go through it many times every day. Our habits that are born and sustained and then die, only to be reborn, are part of the cycle as well. These are the ingrained habits and addictions and behaviors that never seem to end, but go round and round throughout our days: the unhealthy relationships we cannot seem to shake, the patterns of activity and schemas that cause us to overreact to situations or passively accept a condition that's causing us unhappiness. In short, the emotional, dietary, and physical junk that we get rid of only to see it return the next day: this is all samsara.

Conversely, the breaking of the cycle of samsara is enlightenment, or *nirvana*. Within the greatest cycle, nirvana is the ultimate point whereby we remove ourselves from the cycle of birth, death, and rebirth, and no longer experience the suffering and defilement that are the conditions of our being born in the first place. However, just as we experience samsara on a daily basis, so we do nirvana. Nirvana in this case consists of the rejections of the bad habits and the decision not to be caught up in the wheel of defilements. Each time we do this, we experience a minor revelation, a sliver of enlightenment, which makes us a little bit more self-aware and slightly more capable of coping with the greater cycle of samsara.

Therefore, whether you're practicing meditation or attempting to control your impulses and analyzing your dependencies through removing junk from your life, my advice remains the same: pay attention. As you go through the day, observe your own actions and your own behaviors. Stop talking and listen some more; be respectful and hear someone out. Pare back the inessentials and communicate only when you have something to share that's meaningful and thoughtful. Take a breath. Be still. Then you can truly say: Now, we're talking.

4 ❦ Relationships

I've been a teacher for many years and I have have found myself often having to deal with the maelstrom of emotions that many of my students, most of whom are college age, experience on (it sometimes seems to me) an hourly basis. The result of this exposure has been a realization that junk doesn't just only refer to the piling up of stuff in our living area or eating bad food or having too many emails in our computer's inbox (all of which affect young people as well as those who no longer have to cram for exams or juggle homework with a job). Junk can also refer to junk relationships. These are relationships based on unhealthy dependence: whether it's a relationship with someone who treats us badly and who has an addiction that we're enabling, or an addictive relationship that they have with alcohol and drugs that is causing them to behave erratically, irrationally, or self-destructively. Unfortunately, I've also seen that these kinds of problems don't only plague students. They impinge on all of us.

In any relationship there are always at least two dynamics. One is the relationship we have with the other individual—whether it's our boyfriend or girlfriend, spouse, family member, or friend—or thing, a drug or an obsession. The other is the relationship we have with ourselves. Each relationship affects the other; without a healthy relationship with one, we cannot have a healthy relationship with the other. Buddhism offers particular wisdom here: there is a question of mutuality and interrelationship that depends on context. In other words, it's not the relationship *per se* that's the problem; it's in the attachment and attitude toward the relationship that the problem may reside.

Our attitude toward relationships also tends to focus on exclusivity and fixation—as if true love is about concentrating solely on the object of one's desire. But lasting relationships are about giving the other person space and time in which to develop into the person they need to become; they are about allowing a person to follow his or her calling and cultivate his or her individual gifts. Indeed, our most profound expression of love might be letting go of the person we care about. I liken true love to having a hand full of sand. When our hands are extended with the palms opened out, we can hold a large quantity of sand. However, when we ball our hands into fists and squeeze them to hold the sand in place, the sand escapes through the cracks between our fingers and we lose it. Open-handedness is much more likely to hold love than grasping or confining.

Love, therefore, shouldn't be a stifling devotion or possessive desire, but an interaction between two equals who respect each other and who both have a well-defined and solid sense of self. Similarly, it isn't possible to sustain the intense fervor that governs falling in love; no one could continue through their life with that extreme level of dependency on and concern for another. Instead, we fall into what I think is a deeper love: one based on reason, comfort, trust, friendship, companionship, and shared goals.

As we've seen already in this book, Buddhism is very *contextual*. It recognizes that our lives are lived within the stream of time, with many lifetimes before us and many lifetimes after; that our lives impact many beings around us— some of whom we know and some of whom we don't; and that the thoughts we have and decisions we make have a karmic effect that ripple outward like a stone dropped into a pond.

For my students, the relationships that most profoundly govern and trouble their minds frequently involve sex and drugs. Two of Buddhism's fundamental precepts are about abstention from intoxicants and sexual profligacy. In drawing attention to sex and alcohol, the early Buddhists weren't attempting to demonize those who sought pleasure; they were effectively pointing out how we can become attached to both and thus veer off the path to enlightenment. In this context, attachment is similar to addiction, whereby the pleasure has become a compulsion and has thus ceased to be enjoyable.

Sexual attraction is a natural, and indeed necessary, biological urge. But we often confuse sex with the quality of a relationship—as if sex is the sum total of all that we want from a life partner. Relationships involve much more than what we do with each other's bodies; and true physical engagement involves much more than simply coitus or fooling around in bed. What is needed in a healthy relationship is intimacy and respect, both of which might involve sex, or might not. If the quality of the relationship is good, then the healthiness of the relationship will survive no matter the vicissitudes of life or our failing sexual powers. If the quality of the relationship is bad, then it doesn't matter how good are the external experiences of the couple in the relationship—how wealthy they are, how big their house is, or how successful they are in their careers—or how athletic their sex life is. They'll always be unhappy and will always be wounding each other, and no amount of external compensation in material goods or physical pleasures will ever be enough. That's why I believe that it's not necessarily the best thing for two people to remain married to each other; nor do I believe that divorce is always a bad decision. The important issue should be the quality of the relationship and not its appearance.

Likewise, to return to the concept of the relationship we have with ourselves: If we are unhappy with ourselves, or our partner is unhappy with him- or herself, then it doesn't matter how much effort we put into our partnership or how much our relationship is affirmed by our friends, family, or outsiders—our internal relationship will negatively affect the external one. Nor should anyone expect the internal relationship to be healed by a positive external one, or vice versa. They need to be worked on together, to create a virtuous cycle where positive self-esteem leads to a positive external relationship, which in turn reinforces the internal relationship.

Unfortunately, we live in a society that, for all its obsessions with courtship and getting married, isn't very supportive of relationships—either with ourselves or with others. Our society spends its time only interested in romantic love (after all, most Western fairytales end at the wedding)—and then forgets about the couple. In the West, we expect relationships to maintain the same level of passion as when we first met our significant other. We demand fireworks and days and nights of all-consuming physical and emotional intimacy at the same level of burning intensity, rather than enjoying or respecting how a relationship itself can deepen and mellow over the years.

Because in the West we don't invest emotionally in mature or lasting love or valorize it socially or culturally in a way that is honest about the challenges and work of long-term relationships, we treat our external relationships just like the material junk we fill our lives with. We look around for someone new, or younger, or prettier, or wealthier; someone who can enhance our status or power or make us feel we're attractive or potent or young again. We've not learned how to live with each other, to cherish the changes that take place in us as we grow older, and the wisdom and love that develops only over time. Instead, we want instant satisfaction from our partner; if we don't get it, we throw him or her away.

We also find it very hard to be alone. Indeed, we equate being alone with loneliness, when the two could not be further apart. I know of couples who are always together but where it's obvious, from the lack of communication and the way they stand next to each other, that both of them are essentially lonely. And there are others who are always surrounded by people—indeed, they are the life and the soul of the party. And yet they are always in company because they cannot bear to be by themselves. Conversely, I know of people (usually, very evolved souls) who spend a good deal of time by themselves, but who never appear to be lonely. They seem centered and self-dependent, but not self-obsessed or narcissistic. They enjoy other people's company, but they also need to have periods where they can go inside and cultivate their inner selves. Because they understand themselves so well, they are never lonely, even when they are alone.

It is striking that some of the great religious teachers had time by themselves. The Buddha went off alone, and his moment of awakening took place when he was by himself under the bodhi tree. Jesus retreated into the desert where for forty days and nights he was tempted by the devil, who, among other things, promised him the adulation of millions by giving him the kingdoms of the world. Jesus rejected that offer by putting a deeper relationship before it: the relationship he had with God. Jesus sought solitude after he fed the five thousand (see Matthew 14:22–23) and went off alone to pray in the Garden of Gethsemane the night before he died. Moses was alone with God on Mount Sinai when he received the Ten Commandments. None of these great people were averse to large numbers of people: the Buddha had many followers; Jesus spent a great deal of time with crowds and at people's houses eating meals with them; and Moses led an entire people out of exile. But they needed time alone, and it was during that time that they experienced their deepest revelations. The ability to be in silence and to work on ourselves alone might be the greatest relationship we have!

Nowhere perhaps is our throwaway attitude toward relationships more evident than on the Internet and in our celebrity-obsessed culture. While, as I said earlier, the Internet offers an extraordinary array of information that has been made available for more people more easily than at any time in human history, the Web also is full of pornography, slander, videos of people behaving without a shred of self-respect, and a whole range of activities that do nothing but divert too many people from their attempts to lead authentic lives. They spend their time in online chat rooms rather than talking to their partners. They consume pornography to experience virtual sex rather than make love to their flesh-and-blood companions. They watch people making fools of themselves and even produce their own videos so that they, too, can get their fifteen minutes of fame.

The only way I can think about our addiction to stardom and the vicarious pleasures we seek from other peoples' relationship satisfactions or woes is to assume that everyone has a desperate desire to be noticed. Many people seem to feel unnoticed and literally unregarded in their daily lives. They want someone to pay attention to them, even if it's for the most ridiculous and undignified reasons, as if even the momentary exposure to the glare of other peoples' negative judgment about them will make them feel better about ourselves. This is a tragedy, since fame and renown can be as addictive a junk drug as junk food and narcotics. Once you are famous it's hard to release the desire to *keep* being famous. But fame is fickle and, as countless celebrities and others have found to their cost, a life removed from the spotlight once you've experienced such attention can be very hard. You need to be very strong in yourself and aware that many people do not see *you* but see your *image* to resist the depression that occurs when you're no longer in the public eye.

It's a truism that the more you like yourself, the more others will like you; while the more you dislike yourself, the less others will like you. In the last three decades, the human potential movement has burgeoned as people have attempted to make themselves happy through "working" on themselves. The results have been mixed, to say the least. Sometimes I feel as though the effort to develop our potential has merely led to more ways to develop a potential for even more self-obsession. We need to cultivate the contemplative life; and we also need to foster a life of service—where we gain the most satisfaction *for* ourselves by giving *of* ourselves.

When the Buddha experienced enlightenment, he recognized that all life was suffering, that the cause of that suffering was our attachment or craving, that it was possible to stop that suffering, and that there was a path, a Middle Way, not based on asceticism or extreme behavior, and that it could lead to enlightenment. These are the Four Noble Truths and they are the foundation stones of Buddhism. In order to cope with the craving and attachment that causes the suffering, there are six *paramitas*, or perfections, developed by the bodhisattvas. These are ethical behavior, endurance, effort, concentration, wisdom, and, first of all, generosity or *dana*. In our daily lives we tend to think that craving and desire is best dealt with by satisfying that desire. What Buddhism indicates is that it is precisely the opposite: craving is satisfied by being generous and altruistic; when we give away we, in fact, quell the desire. St. Paul relates that Jesus once said, "It is more blessed to give than to receive" (Acts 20:35), and Buddhism has the same principle. While we may not receive a blessing in Buddhism, we will nonetheless be blessed with a fraction less craving and desire and thus be released that little bit more from our burdens.

When I'm asked as a Buddhist nun what my advice for life is—for relationships, for a career, for children, and for old age—it's always the same: "Prepare for impermanence." This should be understood as completely different from thinking of relationships only in the short term and not dedicating one's life to anyone in particular. Far from it. Preparing for impermanence means recognizing that no matter how long we're married for, no matter how faithful we are, or how many or how few children we have, in the end everything passes away. It is inevitable: everything changes; nothing remains the same. The young man or woman we once courted will become an old man or woman. All we need to do is look in the mirror, and look at photographs from twenty years ago. We're not the same. Every day we're losing our hair and shedding our skin cells. Every day food is entering our bodies and leaving it. We grow and change, to be sure. Those skin cells will be replaced and our hair may grow back. But we are not the same.

This should not make us depressed. On the contrary: Far from making us fear every moment of our lives or become heedless hedonists, such a true recognition of the impermanence of all things should sharpen the taste of life and help us savor every moment. Life becomes richer and more intense when we are aware of its evanescence.

Let me give you an example of our attachment to emotions and relationships that are going nowhere, and of how recognizing a facet of impermanence can help. One day, a student came to me whose girlfriend had just called to tell him that she was going back to her former boyfriend. Now I'm a very small woman, and here was this very tall young man and he was crying like a baby in front of me. I asked him what the matter was, and he told me. Life was meaningless, he said, and he wanted nothing to do with the world. He was going to quit the program. So heartbroken did the young man seem that I felt I'd no recourse but to agree with him. "Well, if that's what you feel you have to do," I said. "Then you should."

The more I thought about it, however, the less I liked his decision or my reaction to it. I decided that I shouldn't leave the young man alone and instead should talk to him some more. At ten o'clock that evening, after everyone had gone to bed, I invited the student to my quarters and asked him to tell me what was really going on. He talked to me about his family and his girlfriend and the ex-boyfriend, and after two hours of his talking I offered him some counsel. Eventually, after what was probably another two hours of my counseling, the young man began to brighten and told me that he had to leave my office because he had a lot to do and he wanted to go back and write all those tasks down. The next day he canceled his flight and stayed in the program.

In the space of a few hours the young man's attitude

had changed completely. He'd gone from thinking that life was hopeless to recommitting himself to the program and to the life he'd had before. The conditions of his life were no different than when he'd received the news that his girlfriend was dumping him. It was simply his attitude. He'd realized that what he'd taken for a permanent state of desolation and loneliness was in fact only temporary, and that what was much more important was his self-development and achieving his own goals. Who knows? That man may now be a much more attractive proposition for a woman, precisely because he now has a greater sense of self-worth than he had before.

The concept of impermanence can be hard to grasp. We always want things not to change. We wash our car every day to make it look sparkling and new, and yet one day it will no longer work. Even children grow up and move away from home to start their own lives. Perhaps a daughter doesn't call as often as the parents hoped she would, or a son takes up with a woman whom they think is unsuitable, and they have no say over it. Children go abroad and a spouse dies, and suddenly the parent is alone. These things can shock us unless we've cultivated the mind to recognize impermanence and to acknowledge that the realities of life mean that we're always changing.

We all must go and all relationships—no matter how deep or lasting or meaningful—must come to an end. Similarly, throughout our life we'll run into people who dislike us and whom we dislike. Sometimes it seems we cannot avoid them. In such circumstances, therefore, how wasteful of our time is junk! How much better would our time be spent cherishing what really matters—our love and our friendships with those we care about and who care about us, who treat us well and whom we treat well in return! Why not spend our time on meaningful activity instead of plodding through life doing what we don't want to do? Why not develop depth and substance in our lives instead of skating along on the surface, collecting and discarding? If our time is so precious, and our relationships mean so much to us, then why treat them like junk?

5 ♟ Emotions and Thoughts

Our junk relationships, of course, are often governed by what I might call junk emotions, such as anxiety, jealousy, anger, obsession, short-temperedness, greed, hatred, and so on. These emotions are neither good for us nor are they good for other people with whom we come into contact. These emotions need to be inventoried just like the material goods we have in our closet. It's much harder, of course, to throw these emotions out with the trash, because we've inherited them or indeed have cultivated them over our lifetimes. That's why we need to run an inventory of these emotions as often as we can; to make sure we're in control of them and don't allow them to hold sway over our behavior.

This entails washing the mind. When we come home after a long day, we wash our bodies in the shower. But why

don't we wash the mind—clean it of the impurities and dirt
that have clung to it throughout the day, much as we do the
body? Washing the mind entails releasing the junk of the
emotions, repenting of the misdeeds that we've committed,
and cultivating the virtues of compassion and non-attachment. Healthiness in all things, as well as the removal of junk
in our lives, doesn't just happen accidentally. It needs to be
worked at and cultivated, much as one nurtures a seed in the
ground.

Junk emotions are not simply "strong" expressions such
as anger or greed. They can be "softer" statements of not caring, such as idleness or procrastination or an attitude of in-
difference or boredom. These can, in the long run, be no less
pernicious or addictive. If we're lazy or bored by things, what
does that tell us about how we view our life and the lives of
others? If we can't be bothered to help ourselves, let alone
other people, how can we possibly hope to make any inroads
into releasing ourselves from boredom and idleness? Is it really preferable to avoid risking committing ourselves to
something and making the occasional mistake than be fearful
of change or worried about appearing foolish or overly
earnest? I don't know of anyone who's satisfied by doing
nothing or is fulfilled by being bored. Boredom and idleness
and procrastination are, in my opinion, indulgences that feed
upon themselves until we no longer feel any motivation to
change. Buddhism, by contrast, teaches mindfulness and action: it encourages diligence so that, clearly diagnosing the

cause of *ennui*, we can put effort into action and live a more meaningful life.

Buddhism demands that we're awake all the time to the junk emotions that come about because we don't want to face something. It knows that not confronting the inevitable or dealing with pain doesn't make that pain go away or the day of reckoning not arrive. If, however, we cultivate awareness, if we deal head on with that which is causing us suffering or don't put off what is inevitably going to happen sometime, then we can more easily face our lives with equanimity. This is why we need to develop mindfulness and why our emotions are so essential. If we place our thoughts and emotions in right relation to our actions then we'll more easily fall into healthy and productive habits and become wise users of technology and material goods, rather than be their victims.

We need to examine our emotions and assess how many minutes in a day we feel angry, depressed, anxious, unsatisfied, obsessed, or any other unhealthy feelings. Aren't the minutes where we're consumed by these feelings not junk minutes? For who does anger benefit and who does it hurt? It hurts us. How does feeling unsatisfied help us? It doesn't. When we're obsessed with something or someone, does the object of our obsession care or think about us in the same way? Probably not. As you can see, these feelings are wasted; more than that, they take up the space and time that could be spent feeling more productive and having pleasant thoughts such as love, joy, pleasure, satisfaction, and generosity. Or these periods can be spent in meditation and reflection, deepening the skills and honing the mental discipline that make it easier to control the junk emotions when they're stimulated in our mind.

Unhealthy or junk emotions are the junk food of the mind. We love them because they allow us to wallow in victimhood. We taste the fat of the fear that we are disrespected and gulp down the soda of self-satisfaction. We pour on the sugar of self-abnegation and feeling sorry for ourselves. However, unlike junk food, junk emotions are not as easy to give up and their effects are longer lasting and even more corrosive. Junk food can affect only your own body. But when your body is awash with junk emotions—when we're always angry or dispirited, when we're constantly anxious or perpetually unsatisfied—that can affect everyone around us.

Junk emotions not only belong to individuals. They can be a part of the community or even an entire nation. When a nation holds a negative emotion, such as hatred, toward another country, that emotion can develop into active violence and wars can begin. In some cases it may be hard to determine whether it's the country or the leader who harbors the junk emotions: Some leaders in history have acted from their own anxieties and insecurities rather than genuine fears of being threatened, to launch their countries into disastrous conflicts. This is why it's so important that leaders and politicians are able to deal with their afflictive emotions in a way that is moderate and mindful. That way, countless lives could be saved and much human misery avoided.

These days, there's a lot of discussion about the war on terror. Some people believe that the West and the Islamic world are involved in a clash of civilizations and that there's a global religious conflict taking place. I don't believe that. In my opinion, the conflict is a war of desire, hatred, and delusion. It's one caused by the junk in our minds: the emotions of anger and craving and need. What's needed to stop the war is also in our minds: clarity of thinking, judgment, self-awareness, compassion for sentient beings, and a deep consciousness that ascertains the fears of the combatants and seeks to neutralize them. We cannot fight terror with more terror, or fear with more fear, for this only increases the amount of fear and terror.

This is, of course, very hard. The hardest and most difficult thing we'll ever do is to react appropriately to tragedy. And there are many things in this world that *should* make us feel angry: injustice that allows the innocent to be punished and the guilty to go free, and violence meted out on the vulnerable are shameful things and we wouldn't be human if we didn't feel fury and want retribution. I'm also aware that there is evil in the world and that it needs to be opposed. However, we need to make completely sure that our anger is righteous and not self-pitying or full of our own ego, and that in the actions we undertake we're not simply adding to the violence and cruelty that's so abhorrent to all of us.

Let us examine these junk emotions in more detail. Junk emotions come from embedded presuppositions in ourselves that we project onto the outside world and others. For instance, we may hate someone, not because they're objectively unpleasant as individuals or to us, but because they don't fit our preconceived notions of how we want them to look or behave. Our ideas of looks and behavior might be completely irrational and based only on prejudice and ignorance. Yet we take it out on the other person and accuse them of all sorts of things, as a cover for our own unexamined feelings. One way a junk emotion like anger manifests itself is by making itself so painful that the only way we feel we can get rid of the pain is by expressing our anger. In this way, junk emotions become addictive. The only way we can deal with the anger is to "get it off our chest" by being angry all the time with everybody. Being angry becomes like a "high"—it provides us with the brief satisfaction that a drug does, as everyone recoils from our anger and we find ourselves paid attention to and our anger appeased. But then, sure enough, we "crash," and the anger goes inside again, eating away at us. When we express that anger again, the people around us who felt our anger the first time aren't quite as eager to experience it again, and our friends and family distance themselves from us. In the end, just like a drug, the junk emotion will leave us feeling isolated and alone.

An emotion like anger corrodes in other ways as well. When we're angry we may use foul language. As the phrase suggests, foul language pollutes the air and mind of the person who employs the words as well as the person who hears it. It upsets the equilibrium of people and only communicates anger and distaste. Not only is such foul language junk because it pollutes, but it's also junk because it only communicates negative emotion. As such, it adds nothing except unpleasantness to the world. As was suggested earlier, if we've nothing to say that is positive, then we should say nothing.

Some emotions can be healthy, but when taken to their extreme they become negative. For instance, love. Love is a positive emotion when it's based on respect and care and genuine concern for another's well being. However, love can also turn into attachment, where we're overly dependent on the person whom we're in love with or they on us. Then the relationship becomes unbalanced by power, and that can mean that one partner begins to exploit the vulnerability and neediness of the other. Dedication is also a good emotion: it allows us to stand by someone or pursue an idea or a cause and not be discouraged when things don't work out as we would wish. But dedication can lead to obsession, where we neglect others and ourselves because we're so single-minded, and when we pursue something or someone, losing all perspective on reality.

When love turns into attachment, and dedication into obsession, the individual can become a stalker, a person who won't accept that the object of their affection no longer wants to be with them or convinces themselves that the object of their obsession cares for them or would become their lover. This is all fantasy: sometimes the victim has no idea that the stalker exists until they make themselves a nuisance. Tragically, that emotion of dependence sometimes leads to death, when the person feels that, if they cannot have that person in their life, then no one can. Now, these are extreme emotions, and it's not necessarily the case that attachment will lead to obsession, and that obsession will lead to stalking, and that stalking will lead to suicide or murder. But what is clear is that murder is a result of a chain of junk emotions, and that is why it's important that we break the chain as early and absolutely as we can.

As we see, love and obsession, attachment and hatred are all contained within the same mind and sometimes spring from the same feeling. We may feel that we're possessed by these feelings, we may argue that someone else brings them on or draws them out of us, but the simple truth is that all of them—the positive as well as the negative—come from our mind and our mind alone. That's why Buddhism recognizes how important it is for us to control our minds and to discipline our emotions. The point is not that we cultivate coldness or remove ourselves from feeling anything at all; we wouldn't be human if we did that. The aim of disciplining the mind is to recognize positive and negative emotions and act appropriately. Anger will occur, anxiety will surface, and fear won't be put aside. However, when these feelings inevitably arise, we should be prepared to recognize that emotion for what it is and deal with it before it has a chance to affect us or others. You'll notice that I said that we first have to *recognize* the emotion. This is important, because the mind is tricky and will cover up our junk emotions. Anger might disguise itself as feelings of hurt; fear might disguise itself as wanting to be taken care of or feeling abandoned. We need to excavate those emotions and recognize what lies behind them. Invariably we find a negative emotion that we need to acknowledge and then deal with.

What does it mean to "deal with" a junk emotion? We've already talked about meditation as a tool for dealing with emotions. Yogacara says that we create our own world from our own mind. In other words, the moment that we feel happy or content, we literally create a world of contentment; the same is true of unhappiness or discontent. The mind shapes the world and makes it a reality. Now, of course, this doesn't mean that people who are suffering from hunger, war, natural disasters, and other such tragedies somehow brought the problem on themselves and that if they just smiled then all their problems would vanish. That is absurd and insulting. What it *does* mean, however, is that their attitude to their lives may change to the extent that they might be less weighed down by helplessness and desperation and be able to walk that much further to get help or seek shelter. Perhaps they would encourage others to do the same, and thus save others' lives.

These are, obviously, extreme examples of suffering. However, it's surely obvious that we can change the nature of our reality on an everyday basis. Since it's the mind that tells us whether we feel happy or not, telling the mind to feel happy can *make* us feel happy. Likewise, every time we tell ourselves that we feel unhappy or discontent, we're reinforcing those conditions in our mind, and thus making it that much harder to become content. This is why it's so important to be present to ourselves and tell our mind positive thoughts. Because the mind is both the activator and recipient of our thoughts, we can change how it thinks and our attitude toward those thoughts at the same time.

Another way to deal with junk emotions is to neutralize that junk emotion with something positive. I've found that, in many instances, forgiveness acts as a powerful antidote to negativity. Forgiveness immediately extends a positive emotion outward. We can forgive ourselves for feeling angry and tell ourselves to let the anger go and replace it by feelings of compassion—both for us and the person or situation that made us angry. With the anger neutralized we can then act in a way more appropriate to the situation. Once we remove the junk emotion, it's amazing how not only does the context in which the anger arose change and we can see much more clearly what the correct thing to do would be, but the action we take will be more effective, because it will be devoid of the negative karma that would have attached itself to the action should we have maintained our anger.

This is a very important point to understand. Some people think that Buddhism is a quietist religion, in which one is encouraged to do nothing at all, at the risk of generating karma, which can hold one back from enlightenment. However, as I've suggested throughout this book, it's the *intention* behind one's actions that is important. Everything we do and think and say, as well as everything that we *don't* do or think or say, generates karma, both good and bad. Our karma collects over many lifetimes, and it's a very wise and mature soul indeed who can afford not to generate good karma. Therefore, it's important for us to act in the world, but to do so in a way that we generate as much good karma as we can in ratio to the inevitable bad karma that we'll also produce. Neither good nor bad karma is confined to one single action: both spread. This is why it's vital that the junk emotions are controlled at the source; otherwise, they can extend wider and wider until our single act has caused a world of hurt.

Another very simple way we can monitor our junk emotions is to resolve that we'll not go to bed angry or feeling hateful. I've heard many couples say this is the secret to why their relationships have lasted: they don't go to sleep angry at each other. This means they find the time to talk about whatever it is that's upsetting them, and don't allow themselves to go to sleep (or lie awake unable to sleep) without dealing with the negative emotion. Not only does this mean that the individuals in the relationship are likely to get more sleep and be more rested, and thus not as likely to be in a bad mood the next day; but it means that they can begin that day refreshed and renewed, ready to deal with that day's emotions. Of course, what was said and done the previous day may not be resolved and some difficult and painful decisions may need to be made. But the *negative emotion* will have been removed or reduced, which will make the solution to the problem easier to discern and easier to deal with.

Similar to junk emotions are junk thoughts, which in Buddhism are described as defilements. In other words, they are like garbage. We have already analyzed the junk emotions such as anger and anxiety. Junk thoughts are to some extent the premeditated or even deliberate expressions of those junk emotions. They consist of resentment and jealousy, deceit and spite, flattery and arrogance, shamelessness and parsimony, remorselessness and mistrust. Other junk thoughts are negligence and dissipation, a lack of introspection and being distracted, or in fact any aspect where we act in an ill-considered and thoughtless manner.

As was indicated, the roots of these defilements come from deeper emotions, such as greed or hatred, delusion, egocentricity, doubt, and prejudice. Like junk emotions, junk thoughts are dealt with through cultivating mindfulness. As well as meditation, breathing deeply can help us deal with impure thoughts and unsettling emotions. Breath control has been shown to slow the heart rate and calm the nerves. This in turn can stop the mind racing and the body reacting unnaturally to a situation. It also forces us to think and not to talk, which will give us time to deal more appropriately with someone or something that's upset us. In meditation or while we're breathing deeply, we can even visualize the dispensing of the negative emotion by taking it out to the garbage and dumping it there. This visualization is a technique that actually forces the mind to release the emotion itself.

I conclude this chapter on junk emotions and thoughts with a story. There was a scholar, who was full of knowledge about Buddhism and philosophy and who came to study with a Zen master. As was customary, the Zen master offered the scholar a cup of tea. The scholar was delighted and accepted. The Zen master said nothing and began to pour the tea. However, when the tea reached the rim of the cup the Zen master did not stop pouring. He pointed to the cup of tea in silence but continued to pour the tea into it. "What are you doing?" said the scholar, baffled. The Zen master looked at the scholar. "Scholar," he said. "Take up your cup of tea. How can I pour anything more into it unless you empty it?"

The scholar knew everything there was to know about his religion. In fact, he was so full of knowledge that there was no room for anything else. The Zen master was teaching him, in a very direct way, that he had to empty his mind of all that knowledge in order for him to be able to get the

knowledge he *really* needed, which was to gain enlightenment. I told this story to a group of twelve-year-olds. I later
found out when some of the children went home and heard
their father complaining about how awful his job was or expressing a junk emotion, at least one of them said, "Father,
you need to empty your cup."

What I take from this story is not that we need to become ignorant or not continue to learn about the world, but
that we should stop filling our mind with trivia and junk
emotions that block our path to true knowledge and happiness. We all need to empty our cups.

Conclusion

In this little book I've tried to offer a glimpse of the world of junk that surrounds us and to which we contribute, and offer a few thoughts from a Buddhist perspective. I like to think of this book as a Buddhist literary companion to former U.S. vice-president Al Gore's movie *An Inconvenient Truth*, in that I'm trying to recognize that our lifestyles are leading us toward environmental catastrophe and that we can and need to do something about it. But I'm also trying to point out that our mindset as well as our behavior needs to change. This should be the task of a Buddhist teacher, for Buddhism is full of inconvenient truths!

Once again, I can't deny that I often get caught up in this world as much as anyone, and I have to pull myself back to my center and discipline my mind and remember humility and simplicity. The ways of this world are attractive, seductive, and validated by everything around us; and it's hard to block our ears to their siren songs. What I force myself to remember each day is that at the moment I was born I knew I was very rich already: I had everything I wanted to be able to live a full life. If we recognized how lucky we were from the very beginning, we'd be able to do much more with what we had, wouldn't miss what we didn't have, and would be able to spend much more of our time and energy helping others who don't have as much as we do. And we could do it all from a sense of simplicity, of enjoying every moment and living to the fullest.

Many of us live in great comfort and have a lot to be grateful for. Human beings are very inventive and ingenious creatures. We're developing new technologies all the time that will turn trash into other products and we're finding more efficient and less wasteful ways to use what we have. This is a cause for hope and optimism. I wish I could be as confident about our communication with each other and our thoughts and emotions. Nevertheless, here, too, we each have an opportunity (at no extra cost or expense to ourselves or anyone else, and without using an ounce more energy or natural resources) to generate new and positive thoughts and develop affirming emotions. There is a Buddhist saying: "Transform the defilement into awakening." This should be a principle of all our actions on this planet, whether we're cleaning up pollution in the water, land or air, or whether we're trying to think before we speak and project positive thoughts into the world.

It should be clear from what I've said in this book, how-ever, that no amount of recycling or cleaning up can disguise that we need to create less junk in the first place. We need to practice that mindfulness and awareness so that we save en-ergy by using less of it in the first place. What is important for us to recognize is that in removing ourselves as much as we can from the hurly-burly of consumption and junk we're not denying ourselves pleasure and curtailing the chances for happiness. Instead, we can discover a deeper pleasure, one that redefines what it means to be happy—where life is lived at its fullest, and where every relationship and emotion is rich and complete.

One of the bodhisattvas in the Buddhist pantheon is Maitreya (in Chinese, MiLe Pusa), known as the laughing Buddha. There is a wonderful statue of him at the entrance of the inner courtyard at Fo Guang Shan's Hsi Lai temple in Ha-cienda Heights, California. Like all the other statues, this statue depicts Maitreya with a big belly and round face, laughing up-roariously. Maitreya's name, which is derived from the Sanskrit word *maitri*, meaning "loving-kindness," shows that he repre-sents contentment and abundance. But it's a contentment and abundance that's found not in stuff, but in self-containment and discipline. Indeed, that contentment is located in the *giving away* of stuff. According to the *Maitreyavykarana* or *The Prophecy of Maitreya*, in the translation by Edward Conze, if people and other beings follow the path of Maitreya they will "lose their doubts, and the torrent of their cravings will be cut off: free from all misery they will manage to cross the ocean of becoming; and, as a result of Maitreya's teaching, they will lead a holy life. No longer will they regard anything as their own, they will have no possessions, no gold or silver, no home, no relatives!" And, *The Prophecy* continues: "Theirs will be an abundance of joy and happiness, for they will lead a holy life under Maitreya's guidance."

Joy and happiness unburdened by junk: That sounds like a good life to me!

About the Venerable Yifa

Venerable Yifa has been a nun at Fo Guang Shan Monastery in Taiwan since 1979. She received a law degree from the National Taiwan University, an M.A. in comparative philosophy from the University of Hawaii, and her Ph.D. in religious studies from Yale University in 1996. She was named one of the "Ten Outstanding Young Persons" in Taiwan in 1997. She has been a visiting scholar at the University of California at Berkeley and Harvard University, a lecturer at Boston University, and a faculty member at the National Sun Yat-Sen University in Taiwan. She has also been Dean at Fo Guang Shan Buddhist College and Provost at Hsi Lai University, Rosemead, California. In 2005, she taught at McGill University as the Numata visiting professor, and was until recently Chair of the Department of Religious Studies at the University of the West in Los Angeles. In Bangkok in 2003, she was awarded the United Nations "Outstanding Women in Buddhism Award." Since 2002, Venerable Yifa has conducted the Humanistic Buddhist Monastic Life Program (also called the "Woodenfish Program") for teens and college students, sponsored by Buddha's Light International Society, and more recently has been the director of the Buddha's Light Sutra Translation Center, set up to research and translate Buddhist scriptures. For many years Venerable Yifa has been engaged in interfaith dialogues such as the "Gethsemane Encounter," "International Buddhist–Christian Theology," and "Religious Ethics," supported by UNESCO. She co-chaired "Nuns in the West," an interfaith monastic dialogue, and was a contributor to the "Safe Motherhood Project" by UNICEF's South Asia office. She is the author of *The Origin of Buddhist Monastic Codes in China* (Hawaii University Press, 2002), *Safeguarding the Heart: A Buddhist Response to Suffering and September 11* (Lantern Books, 2002), *Authenticity. Clearing the Junk: A Buddhist Perspective* (Lantern Books, 2007), *The Tender Heart: A Buddhist Response to Suffering* (Lantern Books, 2007), *Discernment: Buddhist Stories on the Conscious Life* (Lantern Books, 2007), and *Sisters of the Buddha* (Lantern Books, 2008).

Also by Yifa:

The Tender Heart: A Buddhist Response to Suffering
978-1-59056-111-9

Yifa elucidates Buddhism's eight different types of suffering from a practical standpoint, illuminating the essential Buddhist ideas of compassion and mindfulness and showing how we can apply these principles to everyday life and in our relationships. Her aim is to help us both reach out to and heal others and protect ourselves when suffering strikes.

Discernment: Buddhist Stories on the Conscious Life
978-1-59056-121-8

In *Discernment: Buddhist Stories on the Conscious Life*, the Venerable Yifa explores some of the central concerns of Buddhism—the nature of suffering, impermanence, the laws of cause and effect, and the nature of the individual—unpacking some of the subtler dimensions of these very popular Buddhist stories. In so doing, she shows how Buddhism relates to contemporary life.

Sisters of the Buddha
978-1-59056-059-4

Like all other world religions, Buddhism has had its share of controversies regarding women's roles. Yifa, a Chinese Buddhist nun, looks at the role of women in early Buddhism, appraises the controversial "eight rules" that women have to obey in order to become Buddhist nuns and examines the social conditions of women throughout the Buddhist world. Yifa concentrates on the still largely unknown Chinese tradition, bringing to light new insights into this important strand of Buddhist culture and the women who were embedded in it. Using her twenty-year experience as a Buddhist nun, Yifa reveals the opportunities and challenges that await any woman who seeks to become a Buddhist, and in so doing uncovers the heart of the spiritual calling.

To order visit www.lanternbooks.com.

Of Related Interest from Lantern Books:

Manifesting God
Thomas Keating, OCSO
Abbot Keating explores what it means to enter the inner room and the transformation that takes place there. It explains the guidelines of centering prayer and offers advice on how to develop the relationship more deeply.

The Common Heart
An Experience of Interreligious Dialogue
Netanel Miles-Yepez, Editor
Here is an extraordinary exploration of the wealth of the world's spiritual traditions combined with dialogue from the heart about the differences and similarities between their paths of wisdom. Participants include Fr. Thomas Keating, Roshi Bernie Glassman, Swami Atmarupananda, Dr. Ibrahim Gamard, Imam Bilal Hyde, Pema Chödrön, Rabbi Henoch Dov Hoffman, and many others.

The Great Compassion
Buddhism and Animal Rights
Norm Phelps
The Great Compassion studies the various strains of Buddhism and the sutras that command respect for all life. Norm Phelps, a longtime student of Buddhism and an acquaintance of His Holiness the Dalai Lama, answers the central questions of whether Buddhism demands vegetarianism and whether the Buddha ate meat. He is not afraid to examine anti-animal statements in Buddhist lore—particularly the issues of whether Buddhists in non-historically Buddhist countries need to keep or to jettison the practices of their historical homelands.

The Green Bible
Stephen Bede Scharper, Hilary Cunningham
"A book of inspiration and transformation for the green-minded, and for those who wish to be or should be."—Matthew Fox

continued

Fruits and Gifts of the Spirit
Thomas Keating, OCSO
The spiritual journey is a gradual process of enlarging our emotional, mental, and physical relationship with the divine reality that is present in us, but one not ordinarily accessible to our emotions or concepts. The spiritual journey teaches us: first, to believe in the Divine In-dwelling within us, fully present and energizing every level of our being; secondly, to recognize that this energy is benign, healing, and transforming; and, thirdly, to enjoy its gradual unfolding step-by-step both in prayer and action.

To order visit www.lanternbooks.com.